THE SPEC SHAMAN

How to Get Your Building Products Specified

Ron Blank, CSI, CDT, **Craig K. Haney**, FCSI, CCS
Brad Blank, CSI

The Spec Shaman:
How to Get Your Building Products Specified

Copyright © 2018 by Ron Blank, Craig Haney, and Brad Blank. All rights reserved.

Cover images copyright © iStockPhoto.com

No part of this book may be reproduced in any form without written permission in advance from the publisher. International rights and foreign translations available only through negotiation with Ron Blank & Associates.

Inquiries regarding permission for use of the material contained in this book should be addressed to:
>Ron Blank & Associates, Inc.
>2611 N. Loop 1604 West, Suite 100
>San Antonio, TX 78258
>210.408.6700

Printed in the United States of America.
10 9 8 7 6 5 4 3 2 1

ISBN: 978-0-9961469-7-5

Credits
Copy Editor	Kathleen Green, Positively Proofed, Plano, TX
	info@PositivelyProofed.com
Design, Art Direction, and Production	Melissa Farr, Back Porch Creative, Frisco, TX
	melissa@backporchcreative.com

TABLE OF CONTENTS

Foreword	5
Introduction	7
Chapter 1 – Building Product Representatives	15
Chapter 2 – Design and Construction Participants	27
Chapter 3 – Getting on the Team	37
Chapter 4 – Project Phases	41
Chapter 5 – Construction Documents	45
Chapter 6 – Product Selection	53
Chapter 7 – Marketing Materials	59
Chapter 8 – Effective Technical Assistance	65
Chapter 9 – Making Effective Product Presentations	79
Chapter 10 – 10 Mistakes Made by Product Presenters	85
Chapter 11 – Office Visit 'Musts'	87
Chapter 12 – Education Equals Specification	89
Chapter 13 – How to Get Specified On LEED v4 Projects	103

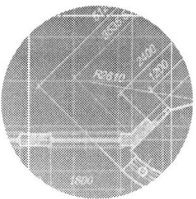

FOREWORD

Without a working background in marketing, it is impossible for design professionals to understand how, why, and when product decisions are made, and how those decisions are incorporated into a construction project. And unless you, as a design professional, have sat on the opposite side of the table from building product representatives, you have no idea the mistakes and misunderstandings that design professionals see every day from marketing staff who call upon them and try to get their products used.

In developing this book, we strived to provide the tools and knowledge necessary so those in charge of marketing all the way through to design professionals will have what is needed so their endeavors bear fruit. This book offers something for everyone, from newly appointed marketing staff to seasoned veterans. It is in fact this latter group's response to our seminars that have often surprised us the most. The information learned from the following pages will be of great use to both the seasoned marketing head who has called on design professionals for years, as well as those just entering the field of building product representation.

This book was written based on our combined 60-plus years of working – with both design professionals and building product manufacturers – to provide insight into the workings of design professionals' offices. Ron Blank of Ron Blank and Associates, Inc. offers multiple very successful programs to assist building product manufacturers in getting their products specified by design professionals, while Craig Haney of IntroSpec LLC has been an architectural specifier for major architectural firms, as well as an independent specification consultant. Brad Blank has developed successful programs for manufacturers to educate design professionals about sustainable aspects of their products, especially LEED. Ron and Craig have been working together for more than 30 years, providing seminars for building product manufacturers on topics that assist them in their efforts, and preparing guide specifications and marketing literature for distribution to design professionals.

By the time you have completed this book, you will have a new understanding of design professionals and how they think and work. That knowledge will make you a better marketer to design professionals; much better than your competitors who do not possess the same knowledge.

Keep in mind that your goal is to get your product specified by design professionals; therefore, read on.

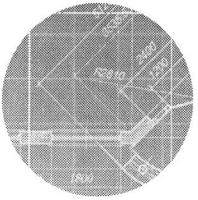

INTRODUCTION

Understand the Process

Providing marketing to design professionals requires a completely different approach than selling athletic shoes or automobiles. Why? First, design professionals quite often make decisions on which products to use, but they rarely pay for those products. It is only in those cases where the design professional and the constructor are one and the same, e.g., design/build firms where the design professional holds the purse strings. The vast majority of design professionals design the project, produce the drawings and specifications, and then take a secondary role of "observer" during bidding and construction. Secondly, unlike consumers who will line up to purchase the latest running shoes, emotions play a very small role in the decision to use a particular building product.

For these reasons, most of what you have learned about marketing may actually be of limited use when marketing to design professionals. You will need to learn a new approach, and this book was written to assist you in that transition.

Understand the Design Professional's Viewpoint

Fees are shrinking: Owners continue to squeeze fees in an effort to maximize profits. In addition, many design professionals work on projects without pay until a construction loan is in place. If the loan never happens, they never get paid. In the past 20 years or so, design professionals have become very protective of their limited time, so getting in the door to see them has become much more difficult. Developing a relationship with the design professionals in your territory is key to opening those doors. We will show you how to do just that.

Deadlines are shorter: Since time is money when a construction loan is ticking, owners exert tremendous pressure on both design professionals and constructors to meet often impossible deadlines. Having the time to meet with building product representatives may not be time they can afford. Additionally, the window of opportunity for presenting your products to design professionals continues to grow shorter. While a design professional might work on a large hospital project for many months or even years, a retail project is a totally different story. There have been instances where big box retailers expect that – from the date they purchase a piece of property for a new store until the building is open for business. However, as little as 4 to 6 months may be allotted. This means that the several months allowed for the design and construction documents to be produced in the past may now be reduced to several weeks. Calling on these design professionals once or twice per year and hoping to hit those few weeks is gambling at its worst.

Lawsuits are rampant: Most design professionals have been sued, often over something that they had no control over. They operated under the theory that the more parties involved, the bigger the payday. Suing a design professional because someone spilled a soft drink on the floor of a mall, and the next person did not see the spill, is much more common than you might think. Somehow that has to be a design flaw. Accordingly, design professionals have become risk-averse, and may not consider using even an excellent product if it has no track record.

Technology is exploding: Consider the number of new products introduced each year, and it is little wonder that design professionalsare overwhelmed. Just the number of single-ply roofing systems on the market today is amazing compared to just 20 years ago.

Decisions, decisions, decisions: It has been estimated that 3,000 product decisions are required on the average building construction project. While some decisions are easy, like whether the Portland cement in the concrete needs to be Type 1 or Type 2, others are extremely complex, requiring detailed research and analysis and possible coordination with other products. There are hundreds of different waterproofing systems available, but which one is best? The answer varies for each project, depending on location in the structure, soil conditions, presence of ground or surface water, initial and life-cycle costs, and a host of other factors. Plus, aesthetic-oriented products present a whole new list of considerations for the design professional. For example, brick for the exterior of a structure might need to complement the color of glazing framing systems, glass, metal wall panels, plaster, stone veneer, and a host of other components. Asking the design professional to change from the red brick of one manufacturer to another might seem easy, but what if the selected brick is a warm red and the proposed brick is a cool red? The entire color palette could be thrown off, requiring the reselection of all other products.

Identify Your Goals

Before you call on a design professional, you must first establish your goals, which differ depending on the project phase. We will discuss project phases in detail later, but for now it is sufficient to say that the earlier or latter phase in a project's life, the less likely you will be to get your product specified.

Early marketing calls to design professionals often focus on introducing yourself, your company, and your products in general. Later in the project schedule, you will focus on getting the design professional to specify your product. Making the wrong type of marketing call at the wrong time is the first problem that uninformed building product representatives will face.

What is your goal? It might seem logical that getting a design professional to specify your product on a project is it, but that is only part of your ultimate goal. (More about this later.) design professionals cannot write you a check or a purchase order, but they can write a specification, which is your ticket into the constructor's office where products are purchased. Getting the design professional to write a specification around your product is the tricky part.

Target the Correct Entities

Calling on the wrong person in a design professional's office is the second problem that you will face.

Design professionals' offices, particularly medium and large offices where you will focus most of your marketing efforts, employ multitudes of people to perform differing functions. Walking in the door or calling on the phone and asking to speak to an "architect" or "designer" will get you nowhere. There are design architects, technical architects, and architects who specialize in marketing the firm's services or following the projects during construction. There may also be interior designers, landscape architects, and various engineers, structural and mechanical to name just two.

In addition to getting the timing of your call right, you will need to learn to identify the decision makers in each office, which varies primarily by the size of the firm.

This book will lead you through the process that design professionals follow on the vast majority of projects, and help you understand who makes decisions, as well as when, why, and what marketing materials you will need. We will teach you the skills you need, from market to design professional – skills that your competitor may not possess.

In order to be successful in your marketing efforts, you need to understand a few fundamental concepts right up front in working with design professionals. These are absolutes, and forgetting even one of them will undercut everything that you have worked for.

Get on the Design Professional's Team

In the early days of architecture, it was not unusual for the architect to be the "Master Builder." He was not only the architect but also served as the engineer and the constructor. Architects were regularly asked to design the structural components, heating, and plumbing system, and often hired and supervised the crews that performed the construction. However, projects were much simpler then. Today's buildings are much more complex. For instance, compare a 1920s two-story brick building where you opened the windows for air conditioning and started a fire in the fireplace for heat to today's high-rise structures that must withstand extreme winds, provide comfort to its occupants in a closed environment, and offer safe egress in the event of an emergency.

As a result of this increased complexity, specialist consultants emerged that the architects now rely on. Structural, mechanical, and electrical consultants are involved in almost every project, but there is an ever-growing list of other consultants as well: interiors, acoustical, landscape, security, audio/visual, specifications, building envelope, hardware, food service, and sustainability, to name only a few.

This means that architects are looking for experts to join their team. It is impossible for them to know everything about all of those 3,000 products, so they look for experts.

This presents the perfect opportunity for building product representatives to get on the team and become the design professional's expert. This is the first "must understand" for building product representatives. Gain the design professional's trust, get on their team, and then do everything in your power to stay on the team.

Get in the Design Professional's Office 'Master' Specification

Design professionals do not write project specifications from scratch. Instead, they use a series of templates commonly called "master" specifications as the basis for their projects. These masters contain most or all of what a design professional needs in writing a specification, and include editing notes and hypertext links to assist them in editing specifications for a particular project. Compare this process to going to your attorney for a new will. They pull out a template, fill in your name and the names of your children, and hit the print button. Design professionals do the same thing.

Earlier we stated that your goal was to get your product specified on a project. But think how much more effective it would be if your product was automatically specified on every project that the design professional issued without any work from you! Getting the design professional to list your product in their office master specification accomplishes exactly this. You can play golf instead of chasing every design professional on every project.

How do you accomplish this? Simply ask the design professional to add your product to their master. If you have worked with them, offered good solutions, and gained their trust, not only will they be willing to add your product but often want to. They know that doing so will help avoid problems during construction.

Stop 'Reactionary' Selling

"Reactionary" selling is waiting for a project to be issued, then calling on the design professional in an attempt to get them to issue an addendum adding your product. Get involved early in the project and get in the specification before it is issued.

Follow the Project

As stated earlier, design professionals typically cannot write you a check or purchase order. You must follow the specification throughout its life in order to close the deal.

You must contact the constructor and any subcontractors or suppliers, who will order products and make certain they have what they need to purchase your product. Stay in touch with them, particularly on large projects where the buyout process could take months or even years.

While you are at it, get on this team as well.

THE SPEC SHAMAN

BUILDING PRODUCT REPRESENTATIVES

Forms of Product Representation

Manufacturers' Sales Employees

Many manufacturers employ a staff to market and sell their products. Manufacturers' employees may have different titles, including sales representative, account manager, sales manager, etc. Regardless of the title they hold, they are responsible for representing the manufacturers' products to design professionals, owners, and contractors.

Manufacturers' sales staff sell a product or perform a service, and they do not sell other manufacturers' products. These salespeople represent the manufacturers, which assume liability for the representatives' actions.

Manufacturers' employees normally receive a salary and some may make a commission on sales. The company normally reimburses them for incurred expenses.

Three types of manufacturer employees include sales, marketing, and technical support.

> **Sales.** Sales employees are responsible for making appointments to present and sell the products. They also call on the architects

to make sure the product is specified, as well as follow up with contractors, subcontractors, and occasionally the owners. They provide pricing information, obtain purchase orders, and arrange for product shipment if requested. Sales employees normally have a sales quota or goal.

Marketing. These employees research the market to determine what attributes, applications, and benefits their products offer purchasing agents and decision makers. Their research evaluates the competition, and then pricing determinations are made to make sales more profitable. Advertising campaigns are established for effective product literature development and sales collateral.

Technical Support. Technical staff answers questions from the design and construction teams and develops product training. Technical support staff does not normally sell. They assist the project team on evaluation, selection, specification, and proper product application. They often provide warranty information, teach, and observe product installation.

Independent Sales Representatives

Independent sales representatives market products for manufacturers through a contract agreement – normally with more than one manufacturer. It is often more economical for a manufacturer to contract for these services than to have an in-house sales force on salary and commission. The independent representative establishes contacts with design professionals and specifiers, contractors, subcontractors, and owners. The agreement between the manufacturer and the independent representative usually stipulates a specific geographical area of activity. The multiple manufacturers' products are usually not competitive.

A manufacturer can quickly start selling in a territory by using established independent sales representatives to market through their contacts. Independent sales representatives derive their income through commissions on sales and are responsible for their own business costs. They have a contractual agreement with a manufacturer. They may be provided a fee to distribute manufacturers' literature or write specifications that include a manufacturer's product. It is also acceptable for manufacturers to pay independent sales representatives a fee for service when pioneering a new product.

Sales for construction projects often require the interaction of independent sales representatives in different geographic territories to work on the same project. When project design occurs in one area and construction in another, the commission on sales is normally split between the representatives in each area. If the product is specified but not used, no commission is paid. Most agreements with manufacturers may include commission based on a percentage of sales from the geographic area or registered projects.

Another form of agreement for independent sales representatives is a sub representative agreement. This form of agreement is contracted between two product representatives, one of whom has a contract to represent a particular product for a large territory but needs help covering another part of that territory.

Independent sales representatives may add different forms of representation. For example, an independent sales representative may have an agreement to be a commissioned representative of one manufacturer and a distributor for another. A manufacturer may hire their own sales force to represent some territories, but independent sales representatives or distributors represent and sell in different territories. These decisions are normally made by the manufacturer.

Architectural Representatives

Architectural representatives are professional educators to architects, specifiers, designers, engineers, and other design professionals such as LEED professionals. An integral part of their job is building long-term relationships with design professionals for their honesty, product knowledge, and availability to consult about the proper products for their projects.

This job often involves frequent travel, meeting with architects and other members of the design team, and attending trade shows, such as the American Institute of Architects (AIA), CONSTRUCT (Construction Specifications Institute), Greenbuild (U.S. Green Building Council), and other trade shows where the audience specifies their products.

Architectural reps represent their company's technology in educational settings such as office visits to specifiers and appropriate design team members, lunch-and-learn (AIA/USGBC) presentations, trade-show seminars, and anywhere they can influence a decision maker to choose and specify their product on a project. They promote new products with guide specifications, BIM objects, technical data sheets, Health Product Declarations (HPD), LEED information, samples, and continuing education (CE) courses. They are always prepared to answer questions, and when they do not have the answer, they always follow up with the information. They are the "go to" professionals for the architects to get information promptly and honestly.

Architectural reps also keep detailed records of every call and provide the follow-up needed. They maintain tickler files of when to call back or when to get the sales staff involved for quotes or technical information. They know the key specifier or decision maker at the firms they call. They make appointments in advance, quite often with a specific product for a specific project at the correct time. They generate leads for the sales staff and coordinate efforts to hold the spec so competitors don't get the project. Architectural reps are product consultants and have technical knowledge that helps inform the architect if their product is right for the project, and if not, who to call.

They use contact management programs to record their progress. They maintain a professional appearance and listen to what the design professional is saying, without interruption. This is a self-starter job that requires time management and appointment-setting skills.

The final goal is to request the company's product and secure it to the firm's master specification, which is then used to prepare numerous project manuals. This means the products listed are specified time after time. architectural reps also work directly with the project managers to have the products specified on specific projects. Product name recognition is promoted. The design professionals specify friends and professionals they trust, so the rep must always be on their mind. The rep becomes the "eyes and ears" for upcoming projects throughout the design stage that have great potential for possible specification.

The architectural representative is one of the most important positions for specification and education regarding the company's products. They plant the seeds, and then the sales staff harvests the fruit.

There is a national architectural representative firm that has architects, engineers, and design professionals who call upon architectural firms for several building product companies at a time. They present a few companies' products to key specifiers at one meeting and educate them about the products' features and benefits through iPad presentations. Their goal is to get those products added to the firm's master specification. Many manufacturers use an independent service because they do not have sufficient staff to send to architects' offices across the country. They want someone with key contacts at the architectural firm who can make a decision to specify the products. Since manufacturers want to lower their marketing costs, using these reps who are extremely effective at getting products specified is an excellent solution.

Distributors

Distributors have agreements with manufacturers to buy, inventory, and resell products to customers. Distributors make a profit on the sale of a product or system; they usually do not work on a commission basis as independent sales representatives do.

Distributors may be stocking distributors who maintain an inventory, or non-stocking distributors who are normally referred to as "dealers." A distributor's agreement with the manufacturer is typically for a specific geographic area and time period. The agreement usually contains a sales objective that is used to evaluate performance.

Geographic areas can be allocated into exclusive or nonexclusive areas. An exclusive territory is one in which the manufacturer has an agreement with a distributor for a specific time when a sole distributor can sell the manufacturer's product in the specific area. For a nonexclusive territory, a manufacturer may decide to contract more than one distributor because of sales potential, or the territory may be too large to be sufficiently covered by one company.

Each distributor has a pricing structure based on volume, credit rating, and level of participation in the sale. Subdistributors may buy from the master distributor or from the manufacturer at a different pricing. Some manufacturers give distributors a significant discount because of the volume of material they inventory.

Combined Efforts

In some cases, the manufacturer will use a combination of the product representatives. The manufacturer may have salaried representatives working one geographic area and manufacturer reps in another, or a salaried manager will oversee the independent reps' activities. Alternatively, the distributor's staff may be performing sales in an area with another rep group helping. This is determined by what the manufacturer believes works for the company.

Qualities of an Effective Representative

Education

How to become an effective product representative is not taught in secondary education. However, there are education courses and accreditation that exist in both Canada and the U.S. for product representatives, including Construction Specifications Canada (CSC) and Construction Specifications Institute (CSI). CSC offers education that leads to a Certified Technical Representative (CTR) accreditation, and CSI offers education that leads to a Certified Construction Product Representative (CCPR) program. These programs indicate that accredited product representatives have a recognized level of knowledge and expertise about the industry and customer needs.

While most representatives probably have attended a college, university, or technical institute, their educational experience could be in any of a range of fields, such as liberal arts, business or marketing, architecture, engineering, or other technical fields. Although a post-secondary education is not a prerequisite, aspiring product representatives will find the knowledge and skills acquired in a technical field valuable in providing a higher quality of services.

Successful product representatives should possess certain character traits, such as:

- interested in the construction industry,
- technically oriented,
- able to communicate effectively,
- eager to help,
- outgoing, self-confident individuals with high self-esteem,
- honest and good ethics, and
- friendly, sociable, and congenial.

To be an effective participant in the construction process, it is important to know the principles of effective product representation and technical assistance. You need to understand the construction process, know the various participants and their needs, be familiar with product literature, have a thorough understanding of construction documents, and have a high degree of professional integrity. Construction product representatives should know how design professionals organize personnel to deliver projects, how and when product selection decisions are made, and who makes them. With this knowledge, the product representative can identify the decision-making individual and deliver the appropriate service at the correct time.

Required Skills and Professional Qualities

There are a number of skills and professional qualities that make for a successful product representative. They include:

- possessing an expertise relevant to the construction products they represent, as well as their interface with adjacent products;
- developing a mastery to understand and market their product; and,
- communicating with others.

The common reference document on any project is the drawings, because they illustrate the extent of work and the details of the project. Drafting lessons can be taken at a technical school or university; however, this formal training must be supplemented by experience in the practical aspects of construction drafting. The product representative must understand contract documents and drawing details, as well as possess the ability to work autonomously.

Construction Methods: Product representatives must understand the practical requirements for on-the-job or factory assembly of the various parts of the construction.

- *Creativity/Adaptability*: A product representative's mind must always be open to new and changing scenarios about the products. Changes are constant as technology develops; therefore, product reps must always be alert to new developments in the industry.
- *Memory*: A good memory is important. Much of the knowledge a product representative acquires is through experience.
- *Computer Technology/Organizational Skills*: All client offices use computers and other electronic devices for storing and reproducing data, and it is important to know which technology will support your sales, for example, Computer Aided Design (CAD) and Building Information Modeling (BIM).

Owners and specifiers rely on written and software resources received from manufacturers and product representatives, as well as other sources. This requires a knowledge of computer technology to support activities associated with promoting a product. Presenting the designer or specifier with product specifications as a promotional tool is the norm. It is important to understand how these tools are used and how to present them.

An effective representative also has an in-depth knowledge of similar building materials marketed and how they function, including:

- ✦ What is the material's relative cost when compared with competitors?
- ✦ Does it possess sufficient strength of the type required for the task at hand?
- ✦ Is it affected or eroded by moisture or air passage?
- ✦ Is it durable?
- ✦ Will it be affected adversely by other products that will be used with it?
- ✦ Has it been used and proven in the field for a reasonable length of time?
- ✦ Has it been thoroughly tested to recognized standards?
- ✦ Does the literature identify product limitations?
- ✦ Will the product meet the life expectancy of the building?

An understanding of the bid period, the period after the award is contracted, the construction phase, after the conclusion of construction, and how the product representative can and should maintain involvement are crucial to being an effective product representative.

Duties and Responsibilities

Making a "sale" depends primarily on the duties required and performed by the product representative prior to and during the bidding phase, and after the order from the contractor. A successful "sale" is not usually considered successful until the project has been bid, the contractor or subcontractor identified, and a purchase order issued for the specified product. Although success of the sales effort ultimately depends on the bid phase, follow-up services play an important role in determining the chances for inclusion into a future project specification. Follow-up services can include following the project's progress, visiting those parties who will be affected by the specified product (such as contractors and subcontractors), and monitoring the installation and subsequent use of that product.

Design consultants and specifiers expect product representatives to have a working knowledge of specifying procedures such as substitutions, alternates, allowances, and unit prices. Some consultant firms maintain a working library of manufacturers' catalogs, and these should be considered an opportunity for future technical service. The representative should anticipate future information needs by providing and maintaining current product data in the library, or supplying it through digital means.

Contractors expect representatives to understand all types of drawings, be able to locate where their product is specified, and understand basic drawing symbols. These skills are necessary in performing the critical function of determining quantity of specified products and verifying proper product application.

At various times, and in various roles as a product representative, the responsibilities will be different depending on the design office structure and project team members. Responsibilities to various members involved in the construction process include:

Design Professionals and Specifiers

In order to be effective in meeting design professionals and specifiers' needs, it is important to have a detailed understanding of the project, including proper information with necessary detail appropriate to the nature or phase of the project. Design professionals and specifiers know that it is impossible for any one person or group to have extensive knowledge of all materials required in the construction industry. They readily acknowledge the need for assistance in selecting appropriate products for their projects. A product representative who exhibits detailed knowledge and competence and has a willingness to consult and a history of honest and ethical dealings, has an excellent opportunity to become an important resource for the design community. Since the product representative will not always be present when design professionals select products, it is essential that design professionals' technical libraries and other reference resources be complete. Maintaining current and complete product literature in the office and online is a continuing challenge for the product representative.

In addition to supplying technical information used for product selection, the product representative may help prepare a specification and provide details for product installation for use on drawings. Product costs, including installation, need to be determined, and the product representative will often be consulted as cost estimates, comparisons, and evaluations are being completed.

Contractors and Subcontractors

Representation services are also provided to contractors and subcontractors. If a descriptive or performance specification has been cited by the contract documents instead of a proprietary specification, the contractor or Subcontractor may select the products from various manufacturers. These product buyers also maintain product libraries requiring up-to-date literature. Clearly defined quotations, assistance in bid preparation, and help in identifying qualified installers are all services that can be provided to contractors and subcontractors. Certain types of product representatives can advise on delivery times and on requirements for proper installation, handling, and storage. After start of the construction phase, assistance may be required in preparing submittals, such as product data sheets, special shop drawings, installation and maintenance instructions, and samples. If the manufacturer prepares submittals, the product representative should help coordinate information with the contractor. The product representative may need to bring in a manufacturer's field representative to observe or supervise installation. These services may be a coordinated effort, or the product representative may perform the on-site observation services.

Owners

Product representatives assist design professionals in product selection and aid contractors in their installation. As ultimate purchaser of the installed products, the owner may require information on operation and maintenance. The specifications may require, or the owner may request, copies of instructions from the product representative and seek advice on operation and maintenance. If replacement parts are needed, the owner may seek information and place an order with the product representative. The representative may be called upon to advise on the operation of installed products, causes of problems, and matters of adjustment and modification. If questions arise regarding warranties, the product representative should be able to provide responsible answers.

Owners who maintain design, construction, and facility management departments rely on knowledgeable product representatives in a manner similar to design professionals. The same is true for government agencies involved in construction because they are often required to use non-proprietary specifications. The product representative will need to assist by helping establish product performance criteria, offering and explaining applicable standards, and providing information on comparable products that comply with the criteria.

DESIGN AND CONSTRUCTION PARTICIPANTS

Today's complex construction projects involve a large number of participants. A working knowledge of each of their functions is critical for the building product representative to effectively market their products and to follow the project after bidding and construction.

These participants are broken down into three groups: owner, design professionals (architect and his/her consultants), and constructor (contractor or construction manager and their subcontractors and suppliers). In general, the lines of demarcation are fairly simple: The owner pays the bills, the design professional performs the design, and the constructor builds the facility.

Owner

The owner of a construction contract is that person or entity who is one of two signatory parties of the construction contract (the other is the constructor). The owner may occupy and use the facility after construction (as in a manufacturer of automobile parts or a hotel) or may construct a facility that will be leased or sold to another party (as in a strip retail center). The owner signs the construction contract, even though they may not be the actual property owner (i.e., a developer who is building a facility for a client for a fee).

The owner is identified in the construction contract as singular in nature, even though it may be an individual, corporation, partnership, or other legal entity.

The owner has certain rights and responsibilities under the construction contract, such as the right to stop the work with or without cause, and the responsibility to pay for completed work. Generally, all correspondence between the owner and constructor either goes through or is copied to the design professional.

Owners vary significantly in their involvement during design, bidding, and construction, from nearly hands-off to controlling the process from start to finish. A doctor looking to build a new facility one time during his/her career is going to rely on the design professional to a great extent, while more sophisticated owners who build multiple large, complex projects will typically employ a project management expert. These owners can exert great pressure on design professionals when it comes to product selections, so they can be a major factor in a project. For example, large hotel chains typically execute national contracts for products like carpet and elevators in order to get favorable pricing, thereby removing the design professional from decisions on those products. It would seem that going directly to these owners to sell your product would be a good idea, but tread lightly here. Many design professionals do not take kindly to a building product representative going "over their head." Always make sure that if you meet directly with an owner, you ask that the design professional also be invited to attend.

Design Professionals

As stated previously, in years past the architect was the master builder, often responsible for design of a facility, as well as its engineering and the design of its mechanical systems, and perhaps, even the construction. Due to the complexity of modern construction, the design and construction process requires many design professionals. Some of these need to hold licenses to practice in their respective fields (Structural engineers, for example), while others may simply have expertise in their chosen field (acoustical consultants). A large, complex project may have as many as 20 or 30 design professionals working on it at various times. As a general rule, all of these will be coordinated by the architect, but some owners or project managers perform this function as well, especially on more complex projects.

The Architect

The architect is the person or entity licensed to practice architecture at the project locale and is responsible for the overall project design, which involves adherence to the owner's requirements, the project's aesthetic approach, building-code compliance, and life/safety issues. The architect must meet the owner's program requirements, design the facility in accordance with applicable codes and ordinances, and deliver a facility that meets the owner's budget. While the architect is typically identified in the construction contract, it is only because he/she has third-party obligations. Rarely does the architect sign the construction contract.

Before you can call on an architect, you will need to understand the magnitude of the office that they work in. Architects' offices vary greatly in scope, which is mostly a function of the type of projects they work on.

> **Small offices**: These offices typically include from 1 to 10 people, and they often work on residences and other smaller-scale projects. Consequently, smaller offices may not be worth pursuing, as they can be numerous and consist of someone working out of a spare bedroom. If they call you, by all means follow up, but otherwise, don't waste your time. Some large metropolitan areas can have 300 to 400 architect offices. Smaller firms represent about 80 percent of all architectural firms, so you can see what a huge effort it would take to contact all of them in your area and, subsequently, receive an insignificant return on your investment.

Mid-size Offices: Often employing 10 to 50 people, this size office should be high on your list of calls to make. They represent from 15 percent to 20 percent of all architectural firms, and are responsible for a large number of substantial projects. Their projects often include everything from churches, auto dealerships, retail centers, and schools to major interior finish-out projects, such as corporate headquarters and law offices.

Large Offices: These firms can have up to 1,000 employees, and often have offices in multiple locations. It is not unusual for them to also have in-house engineers and interior designers and one or more specification writers. Representing less than 5 percent of all architectural firms, they are responsible for mid- and large-scale projects, including major hospitals and sports venues.

Identifying decision makers in these various offices can be tricky, but there are some basic guidelines:

Small Offices: Since the number of employees is so small, finding the decision makers is pretty simple: Locate the owners or partners. These firms will often only have one or two partners, a part-time bookkeeper, and a few CAD/BIM operators (more about these later), so the owner or partners are the only ones qualified to make product decisions. Identifying the owner or partners is sometimes really easy: Architects often include their names in the firm name, so just look for "Smith and Jones Architects" and ask for one of them.

Mid-size Offices: Now your task gets harder. Not only are the partners' names often not on the door, but this size of firm can include a multitude of different job functions, including partners, project managers, project architects, designers, CAD/BIM operators, and perhaps a specification writer. Partners are often responsible primarily for finding work, which they then turn over to a project manager, who is responsible for the project from start to finish. Project managers will have designers, project architects, and others working under them, but they will always know what phase a project is in and who is working on it. They are key players. Additionally, these firms may employ a specification writer, who can be your best friend because not only do specification writers write specifications for products, they also make product recommendations and can open the door to meeting with designers and project architects.

Large Offices: It can be daunting to approach one of these firms, especially when they have made a name for themselves and work out of multiple floors in a downtown high-rise, so take this elephant one bite at a time. Many large offices work on what is called a "studio concept," such as a retail studio, hospitality studio, and sports studio. Think of them as firms within a firm with their own partners, designers, and project managers. If your product is not suited for one of these studios, then eliminate that group from your marketing efforts and focus on the ones that have a higher probability of being a good fit. Also keep in mind that large firms often have multiple offices. Don't make the mistake of assuming that just because one office is specifying your products that the others will as well. Sometimes the only contact between offices is at the partner level, and partners rarely make product decisions. If you have multiple locations for one firm in your territory, call on all of them.

Engineers

The architect knows that the term "engineer" includes a broad range of consultants who are each responsible for one aspect of the project as it relates to their area of expertise. Typical engineers who show up on architectural projects include structural, mechanical/plumbing/electrical, and civil, but there are others.

As a general rule, engineers' offices are smaller than architects' offices, and they typically work for multiple architects on a revolving basis as needed. It is rare to find either a designer or a specification writer in an engineering firm, as these tasks are usually performed by the engineer working on each project. Finding the responsible party in an engineer's office is pretty simple as long as you identify the responsible engineer. If you are in contact with the architect on a project, simply ask who their engineers are.

Interior Designers

Many architects work with separate interior designers. These firms are responsible for the interior finishes but also work with the architect in laying out interior spaces. Designers may also work with the owner in selecting what is referred to as "FF&E" – fixtures, furnishings, and equipment, which can include everything from chairs and tables to systems that incorporate movable partitions and furniture.

Additionally, many interior designers work on projects that do not include an architect's services, such as the interior finish-out of a full-floor law firm. As a result, you will need to track down these firms apart from the architects you are working with. Some of these firms are national in scale with multiple offices and work on very large projects.

Other Consultants

Complex projects can include consultants for landscape, lighting, audio/visual, acoustics, food service, security, sustainability, cost, building envelope, and specifications, to name just a few. It is not unusual for a large, complex hospital to have 30 or more consultants.

Since their work is highly specialized, there are far fewer of these consultants than architects, but they are easier to find. Just look online or ask the architects whom you are working with.

Specification consultants present a unique opportunity for building product representatives. These firms are typically small (one to four employees) but work for many architects during the year. It is not unusual for a specification consulting firm to work on more than 100 projects per year, working with 30 or 40 different architects. Yes, they write project specifications, but they are also considered valuable resources when it comes to products. Consequently, specification consultants are often asked to recommend products that have certain characteristics or proven track records. While they probably will not select the high-performance glass for a building's exterior, they are commonly asked which firms manufacture glass of a certain color with a certain shading coefficient. For these reasons, specification consultants can be your best friend. They not only specify your product, but they also open doors for many architects as well. There are only about 100 of these firms in the U.S., so you would think that they would be the hardest to locate, but that is not true. Most of them belong to the specification consultants in Independent Practice (SCIP), which has a complete list of members on its website.

Constructor

The vast majority of projects are constructed by an entity other than the design professional. The constructor is a signatory party to the construction contract and is responsible for all or designated portions of the project. They execute subcontracts for specific portions of the work and coordinate the work of all subcontractors under their umbrella. As a result, they are ultimately responsible for deciding which products are used on each project. While the design professional specifies products, the constructor is the one paying the bills, and they can exert huge pressure on final production selection. Consequently, you must be in touch with the constructor after a project is issued by the design professional. Always remember: Design professionals write specifications, but constructors write checks.

Enormous projects can be set up on a "multiple prime contract" basis, where two or more constructors typically work on the project at the same time. A common example would be a large hospital where a general contractor, mechanical contractor, and electrical contractor would all hold contracts directly with the owner. Needless to say, this approach requires careful coordination by the owner or an owner-employed project manager, resulting in cost savings to the owner by eliminating the markup that would otherwise be added to mechanical and electrical contractors working under the general contractor.

The constructor can take on many roles, as determined by the owners' needs. Less sophisticated owners will want a constructor who handles everything, while owners who construct multiple, large, or complex projects may take on some of the duties themselves. Here are the most common types of constructors that you will encounter:

> **Contractor**: The traditional method of constructing a project is to use a contractor (general contractor). Contractors may or may not have their own workforces but are responsible for the overall project. Contractors may be hired by direct negotiation or by competitive bidding. Direct negotiation is often the approach used on privately funded projects while competitive bidding is typically required if public funds are involved. One variation is for the owner to hire the contractor based on qualifications, not price, and then have the contractor competitively bid the subcontracts.
>
> **Construction Manager**: Similar to a contractor, these entities rarely have their own workforces; all work is executed by subcontract. Similarly to a contractor, they are often hired by the owner based on qualifications and then bid out subcontracts. One huge advantage of working with a construction manager is that, unlike a hard bid scenario where the work is designed and issued for bids only to find out that the cost is too high for the owner's budget, a construction manager can do "what if" scenarios wherein the design professional can ask for prices on multiple systems such as the exterior skin before the design is finalized and the construction documents completed.
>
> **Design/Builder**: In this scenario, an architect and constructor work together to bring a project in on time and under budget by a single contract. The architect may be a separate entity that has signed a contract with the constructor for a particular project, or may be an integral part of the constructor's office, pursuing multiple projects.

The constructor is identified in the construction contract as singular in nature, even though it may be an individual, corporation, partnership, or other legal entity.

Subcontractors and Suppliers

Nearly every construction contract relies on subcontractors and suppliers to perform much or all of the work. As a general rule, these parties do not sign the construction contract but are bound to its terms by their subcontract with the constructor. Subcontractors typically perform the actual work, while suppliers furnish materials only.

Project Manager

A project manager is an entity hired by the owner to assist in seeing a project to completion where the owner has neither the time nor the expertise to do so. A project manager's role can vary quite a bit from project to project. On a smaller-scale project, they may coordinate various entities, including the architect and constructor, approve payment applications, and, in general, watch out for the owner's interests. On more complex projects, they can also be involved in interviewing the architect and consultants, as well as the constructor.

THE SPEC SHAMAN

GETTING ON THE TEAM

Many people falsely believe that design professionals are all-knowing and all-seeing. Nothing is further from the truth. Design professionals cannot know everything about the huge number of products and systems required to complete a construction project. Instead, they look for qualified people to assist them. People like you.

Getting on the team requires that you accept several facts:

- ✦ It will take some time to gain the design professional's confidence. This is not a short-term effort; it can take years to work your way into the design professional's good graces, but once you do, you will be his/her unpaid consultant for years to come. Unpaid by the design professional that is, since your reward will be specifications for your product that can be taken to the constructor and exchanged for a check.

- ✦ You will not be "selling," and if you try to do so, you will quickly be dropped from the team. Your job is to educate and assist in product selection so that specifications can be written. Sometimes you will be forced to recommend your competitor's product, but that is perfectly acceptable. Design professionals will value your honesty and ask you back for the next project. Slow and steady wins the race.

Your goal is to make yourself the design professional's expert and "go to" person. You may find them asking you to recommend someone to assist them on products that you do not represent. This is wonderful, because now they trust you.

Two of Craig's personal experiences perfectly illustrate this concept:

The Good Product Representative
"As a young design professional, I took over the specification writing duties for an architectural firm. The previous specifier came to me one day and asked if I wanted to have lunch with him and a product representative. The representative seemed like a very reputable fellow representing good products, and I kept his card for future use.

"A month or so later I called him, proudly stating that I had a use for one of his products and had some questions for him. After I explained our needs, there was silence on the other end of the line. When he finally spoke, he said, 'Let me get you my competitor's phone number. This is not the correct use of our product. Call me on the next project.'

"Needless to say, I was a bit set back, but this fellow has become my go-to person, reaping the rewards of many, many projects that I have specified his products on."

And the Bad One
"While working as an in-house specifier for a large firm, I was approached by one of the firm's project designers and asked to specify a product for a current project. This product was to be used in an exterior application, but it appeared to me that it might not perform as expected on the exterior of a building.

"I asked the designer if he had checked on this aspect of the product, and he assured me that he had. When I asked who had told him that an exterior installation was acceptable, he responded that the local representative had. I asked who that person was, and my fears were confirmed when the designer named was someone that I knew from previous experience, and he would say nearly anything to get a sale. I asked the designer to please arrange a meeting with the local representative at our office.

"During the next few days, I was able to reach a technical adviser for the manufacturer of the product and ask him whether or not this product was suitable for exterior use. He responded, 'Absolutely not! It will delaminate and change color!'

"When I sat down with the local representative and the designer, I asked the representative whether this exterior installation was an acceptable use for this product. He stated that it was. I asked him to leave and never return.

"He tried several times over the ensuing years to get back in good standing with me, but I refused to even take his phone calls. Why would I want to trust someone who could have cost my firm a huge amount of money for litigation expenses and replacement costs?"

Get on the team, then work hard to keep that position. Never compromise, no matter how large the potential profit, and you will leave your competitors in the dust.

THE SPEC SHAMAN

chapter four

PROJECT PHASES

As a general rule, design projects follow a specific path, which is described in the American Institute of Architects' (AIA) "Standard Form of Agreement Between Owner and Architect." It creates the basis for many design contracts and has been plagiarized many times.

The building product representative will be interested in five project phases that will affect their marketing efforts, but first we need to examine the distinction between a "design-oriented" and a "technically oriented" product. Design-oriented products are those that have a major impact on the project's aesthetics, such as high-performance exterior glass, brick, metal panels, and stone. These products are typically selected earlier in the project than technically oriented products. A technically oriented product is one that does not significantly impact the project's aesthetics, but is required to make the project function correctly. Technically oriented products include things like floor coatings and joint sealers, and are typically selected later in the project. Make sure that you understand where your product fits in, as trying to approach a design professional with a product at the wrong time will prove to be a waste of time.

These are the five project phases that the building product representative needs to understand. Learn the acronyms, as design professionals use them frequently.

Schematic Design (SD): An early design phase in which the design professional looks at things like site layout and basic building layout. This phase represents approximately 15 percent of the design professional's fee, so it is not one of the longer phases. While the design professional may begin looking at basic building materials during this phase, they typically do not look at or select specific products. They will explore whether the exterior walls will be brick or metal panels but not which manufacturer's brick. The building product representative's role in this phase is to ascertain what materials are being considered. If those include your product types, be ready to assist in product selection during the next two phases.

Design Development (DD): During this phase, which represents approximately 20 percent of the design professional's fee, the design developed under the SD phase and approved by the owner will be refined and developed into more detailed documents. These will be developed further in the next phase and may be issued for preliminary pricing by a constructor or cost consultant. Product decisions made during this phase are primarily limited to design-oriented products that have a major impact on building aesthetics, both exterior and interior. If your products fall into this category, then you should be calling on the design professional at this time. Technically oriented products will be selected during the next phase. Attempting to get the design professional to look at a technical product at this point is pretty much a lost cause, as they have too much to do and too far to go before they need these products.

Contract Documents (CD): Under this phase, the design will be turned into documents suitable for bidding/negotiation and construction. All product decisions will be made by the end of this phase, so no matter what your product is, you need to have it in front of the design professional by midway through this phase. This phase represents approximately 40 percent of the design professional's fee, making it the largest but not the longest phase. Documents issued by the design professional during this phase include the drawings and the project manual, which includes not only specifications for materials and systems but also bidding and contracting requirements.

Bidding/Negotiation (BN): This is the phase when the bidding documents are issued to constructors, either for competitive bidding or direct negotiation, and represents approximately 5 percent of the design professional's fee. It is also the shortest phase, running from 3 to 6 weeks on a typical project. This phase may also include the development of pricing alternatives and value engineering to reduce costs. Value engineering is a term used to describe the process of allowing the submittal of options that will reduce costs while still giving the owner a successful project. A typical value engineering proposal may be for the use of individual air conditioning units in lieu of a central cooling tower system; hence, the air quality results should be the same, but the operation and maintenance costs may be higher. The only documents produced by the design professional during this phase are addenda, which are used to modify and supplement the bidding documents.

Contract Administration (CA): This phase represents approximately 20 percent of the design professional's fee, but it is the longest phase, running throughout the construction period, which can last from 1 to 5 years, depending on the size of the project. The design professional's involvement during this phase includes the review of the constructor's submittals, such as shop drawings and payment applications, and site observations of the work as it progresses. Documents issued during this phase include change orders, which are used to modify construction cost or construction time, and supplemental instructions or field orders, which are used to document modifications that do not affect construction cost or construction time.

THE SPEC SHAMAN

CONSTRUCTION DOCUMENTS

Bidding Requirements

These are used to attract prospective bidders and give them information necessary to prepare and submit a bid. They typically include:

Advertisement or Invitation to Bid: This document includes information such as names of the owner and architect, bid date and time, how bidders can obtain bidding documents, information about site examination, and a preconstruction conference if applicable. The Advertisement for Bids may be published in local newspapers and other outlets as required by competitive bidding laws.

Instructions to Bidders: These contain information on how to fill out and submit a bid, including number of copies, information on bid bonds, affidavits, and other required documentation.

Bid Form: This is the actual form used by bidders to submit their bids.

Bid Form Supplements: These can include forms such as bid bonds, non-collusion affidavits, and others that must be submitted at the time of bidding.

Contract Forms and Conditions of the Contract

The Contract Form includes the actual form of the contract between the owner and constructor, which may be a standard form offered by the American Institute of Architects (AIA), Engineers Joint Contract Documents Council (EJCDC), Design/Build Institute of America (DBIA) or others, or may be a custom document prepared specifically for each project.

General conditions expand on the general clauses in the contract form, and form the link between the contract and the specifications. These are often standardized documents such as the AIA's "General Conditions of the Contract for Construction." They cover topics such as duties of the various parties, insurance requirements, payments, and completion.

Since the general conditions are often standardized documents, they cannot cover every condition for every project, hence, the need for supplementary conditions to cover project-specific requirements. For example, while the general conditions may require that the constructor carry property insurance, the limits vary between projects and must be covered in the supplementary conditions.

Subcontractors and suppliers are typically held to the same requirements as the constructor via clauses in their subcontracts, so make sure that you understand what you will be held accountable for.

Drawings

The AIA General Conditions of the contract state that "the drawings are the graphic and pictorial portions of the contract documents showing the design, location, and dimensions of the work, generally including plans, elevations, sections, details, schedules and diagrams."

The same document also states that "the specifications are that portion of the contract documents consisting of the written requirements for materials, equipment, systems, standards and workmanship for the work, and performance of related services."

Think of drawings as showing quantity, while specifications show quality.

As a general rule, drawings:

- ✦ Are one component of the contract documents upon which a construction contract is based.
- ✦ Are typically arranged according to design discipline, with civil first, landscape next, then architectural, structural, mechanical/electrical/plumbing, etc.
- ✦ Should never be scaled to ascertain quantities, as they may not be entirely accurate. Calculations from dimensions indicated on drawings are necessary to obtain accurate cost estimates.

Project Manual

The term "Project Manual" is used by design professionals for that volume that includes the bidding requirements, agreement, conditions of the contract, and specifications, and can be revised after bidding to include Addenda. It does not include drawings or contract modifications, which are made after a contract is executed.

The Project Manual is organized to include introductory information such as the title page, certifications page, and table of contents, bidding requirements, contracting requirements, and specifications.

Let's look at how specifications are organized:

MasterFormat

This document, issued jointly by the Construction Specifications Institute (CSI) and Construction Specifications Canada (CSC), organizes specifications into logical groupings of construction information such as concrete, masonry, and metals. It is used throughout North America and in other areas of the world, and is what many people refer to as the "CSI Format." It organizes specifications into Divisions, which are fixed in number and title, e.g., "Division 04 – Masonry". This approach allows for easy scanning when looking for specific information, since specifications are not read like a book from cover to cover.

2016 MasterFormat Division Titles

Procurement and Contracting Group
- Division 00 – Procurement and Contracting Requirements

Specifications Group
- General Requirements Subgroup
  - Division 01 – General Requirements
- Facility Construction Subgroup
  - Division 02 – Existing Conditions
  - Division 03 – Concrete
  - Division 04 – Masonry
  - Division 05 – Metals
  - Division 06 – Wood, Plastics, and Composites
  - Division 07 – Thermal and Moisture Protection
  - Division 08 – Openings
  - Division 09 – Finishes
  - Division 10 – Specialties
  - Division 11 – Equipment
  - Division 12 – Furnishings
  - Division 13 – Special Construction
  - Division 14 – Conveying Systems
  - Divisions 15 thru 19 – Reserved
- Facility Services Subgroup
  - Division 20 – Reserved
  - Division 21 – Fire Suppression
  - Division 22 – Plumbing
  - Division 23 – Heating, Ventilating, and Air Conditioning
  - Division 24 – Reserved
  - Division 25 – Integrated Automation
  - Division 26 – Electrical
  - Division 27 – Communications

Division 28 – Electronic Safety and Security
Division 29 – Reserved

Site and Infrastructure Subgroup
Division 30 – Reserved
Division 31 – Earthwork
Division 32 – Exterior Improvements
Division 33 – Utilities
Division 34 – Transportation
Division 35 – Waterway and Marine Construction
Divisions 36 thru 39 – Reserved

Process Equipment Subgroup
Division 40 – Process Integration
Division 41 – Materials Processing and Handling Equipment
Division 42 – Process Heating, Cooling, and Drying Equipment
Division 43 – Process Gas and Liquid Handling, Purification, and Storage Equipment
Division 44 – Pollution Control Equipment
Division 45 – Industry-Specific Manufacturing Equipment
Division 46 thru 47 – Reserved
Division 48 – Electrical Power Generation
Division 49 – Reserved

SectionFormat

Also jointly issued by CSI and CSC, this document provides a framework for organizing the text within a specification section, which describes a particular material or system and its installation. Sections do not necessarily relate to a particular trade or subcontract, although they often do. Each section is identified by a six-digit code, e.g. "04 20 00 – Unit Masonry" according to MasterFormat. The first two digits always refer to the Division, in this example Division 04 – Masonry. Within each section, specification text is organized under three headings, again allowing for fast scanning of desired information.

2009 SectionFormat Headings:

Part 1 – General
    Summary
    References
    Definitions
    System Description
    Submittals
    Quality Assurance
    Delivery, Storage, and Handling
    Project/Site Conditions
    Sequencing/Scheduling
    Warranty
    System Startup
    Owner's Instructions
    Commissioning
    Maintenance

Part 2 – Products
    Manufacturers
    Existing Products
    Materials
    Manufactured Units
    Equipment
    Components
    Accessories
    Mixes
    Fabrication
    Finishes
    Source Quality Control

Part 3 – Execution
    Installers
    Examination
    Preparation
    Erection
    Installation
    Application
    Construction
    Repair/restoration
    Reinstallation
    Field Quality Control
    Adjusting
    Cleaning
    Demonstration
    Protection
    Schedules

When looking in a project manual for a specific product, you can skip a lot of inapplicable text. For example, if your product is masonry accessories, go to Division 04 – Masonry, Section 04 20 00 – Unit Masonry, and look under Part 2 – Products.

Contract Modifications

Contract modifications are issued after a construction contract is executed to modify or supplement the original documents due to changes or when clarifications are needed. They consist of two types:

- **Construction Change Directives and Field Orders**: These are used to incorporate changes and clarifications that do not affect construction cost or construction time. Examples might include instructions to move a light switch 6 inches to the left, or that a particular dimension is to the face of studs and not face of drywall.

- **Change Orders:** These are used to incorporate changes and clarifications that do affect construction cost or construction time. They can range from the simple, such as to add a second coat of paint on the north wall of Lobby 100, to complex, such as to change the heating system from individual units to a cooling tower system.

PRODUCT SELECTION

In order to have any hope of getting their products specified, Building product representatives need to understand how design professionals think. Selecting a building product is not like selecting a new automobile, for example, because there are no emotions involved.

The design professional makes selections based on a known set of parameters. General product considerations can include:

Is this a new or time-proven product? While many designers want the most recent product used on their project, most owners or partners of a design professional firm want something that they know will perform and not cause problems, therefore avoiding lawsuits. They are, after all, paying the premiums and deductibles for the firm's professional liability insurance, which can be ridiculously high and increase with each new lawsuit.

Is the product suitable for its intended purpose? Using an interior product on an exterior location can have drastic consequences. Even something as seemingly innocuous as taking a glass curtain wall designed for vertical uses and tilting it 45 degrees, thereby turning it into a sloped glazing system, can result in major water leakage.

Is the product used in traditional ways or is this a unique installation? Installers obviously perform better when they are familiar with a product and its installation. Asking them to deviate from normal construction practices could be disastrous. This effect is amplified when a project includes conditions that the installer is not familiar with or equipped to deal with, such as installing the product on the exterior skin of a 50-story high-rise versus a single-story school.

Is the item available at the project location at the required time? Having a wonderful product is great, but if it is not available in time to meet the construction deadline, it is of no use to the design professional or the constructor. Therefore, be prepared to inform the design professional when it might be time to look at an alternate product if your product's delivery could be delayed.

Who distributes, installs, and maintains the product? Design professionals would love for one entity to perform all three, but that rarely happens. However, the professionals want to know if the item is available in their locale, whether it needs to be installed by a certified installer, and if the owner's maintenance personnel can maintain it or if it requires factory-trained personnel.

Are there equivalent products? Every construction product manufacturer that we have ever met wants an exclusive specification for their product, but that rarely happens. On publicly funded projects, it typically violates open and competitive bidding laws to close a specification, except when matching existing products or when it can be proven that no other product will do the job. Even on privately funded projects where closed specifications are allowed, most owners discourage them under the theory that competition lowers costs. Unless the owner is a major consumer of construction products with national contracts in place, we rarely see closed specifications.

Is the product compatible with other products on the project? Not all products play well with other products, and disaster can result. This is particularly true of products like joint sealers, waterproofing, and coatings that arrive at the jobsite in a bucket and have to be applied and allowed to cure.

Is the product sustainable? In this day and time, sustainability is more than a buzzword or something that people like to brag about. With the introduction of the LEED (Leadership in Energy and Environmental Design) rating system by the U.S. Green Building Council, a new chapter in construction in North America was ushered in. Achieving LEED certification for a building originally involved bragging rights and marketing but soon evolved into a project requirement imposed by an owner or public entity. In some cases, constructing a project without LEED certification became impossible. Since then, other sustainable rating systems have popped up. Sustainability is no longer a fad. Unfortunately, in their zeal to show that their products are sustainable, many building product manufacturers did themselves a huge disservice. Due to a lack of understanding of LEED and other sustainable rating systems, they often made claims that were either misleading or totally false. For example, LEED gives a credit for using products containing recycled content, but not just for using these products. There are qualifications on type of recycled content, and the values apply to an overall project goal of 10 percent or 20 percent recycled content. Some building product manufacturers falsely claim that their products are "LEED Certified." Products are not certified; projects are. Design professionals even came up with a term for this misleading marketing: "greenwashing." Sustainable requirements are constantly evolving, so make sure that you are current with them.

Best product versus best product for the project: When design professionals are working for a developer or other budget-conscientious owner, arguing that your product is the best one available – but at a higher cost – is often a wasted effort. A developer just wants the door hardware to not fall apart until they flip the project. Save those arguments for the project where the owner intends to occupy it for a long period. Save yourself a lot of aggravation and the design professional heaps of time.

Other selection considerations can include:

Aesthetic Issues: Architects are very design-focused, and choosing between an aesthetically pleasing product and one that performs as well but is considered less appealing can be a major consideration. Besides, when it comes to building exteriors and major interior spaces, each product must be carefully considered in conjunction with every other product. While your red brick might seem the same as the one the architect has selected, yours might be a warm versus a cool red that does not work with all of the other products already selected.

Performance Characteristics: Since design professionals are the first ones to get sued when something fails, they are especially concerned about how a product performs. A product that does not meet the requirements of the building code or that fails prematurely under normal use and exposure will be avoided at all costs.

Installation: A product that can be easily installed can be much more alluring to design professionals than one that is difficult to install. Many tradespeople on a construction project have limited education and experience, so the easier the installation, the higher the likelihood of success.

Safety: Design professionals are typically not that concerned about jobsite safety since they have very limited exposure to liability. But they are very concerned about fire safety, life safety, and physical safety after installation. Building codes dictate fire and life safety requirements, and there are very few options that can be used. As for physical safety, many a design professional has been sued because someone slipped and fell after a soft drink was spilled on the lobby floor of their project.

Accessibility: Beginning with the Americans with Disabilities Act (ADA), design professionals were thrust into accessibility in a whole new way. Since then, many states and municipalities have developed their own standards for accessibility, and the design professional has no option but to comply with any applicable standards.

Durability: Placing a floor tile designed for residential use inside the entrance to a major mall would be foolish, as the high volume of traffic coupled with tracked-in dirt and grit would certainly cause the tile glaze to fail. But durability has many other aspects as well: freeze/thaw resistance, ultraviolet resistance, and resistance to pollutants, to name just a few.

Cost: Cost considerations take two forms: initial cost and life cycle cost. While design professionals must consider initial costs in order to bring a project within the owner's budget, they must also consider how a product performs throughout its useful life.

Manufacturer's History and Reputation: There is no substitute for being a reputable company in the eyes of a design professional. Far too many construction product manufacturers have learned the hard way that refusing to repair or replace a product, even if the circumstances are questionable, can have a huge, negative effect on their bottom line. Sending free replacement products can mean the difference between saving relatively few dollars on one project and never getting specified by that design professional again.

Warranties: Product warranties can be a very sensitive subject with oesign professionals. While most owners want as long a product warranty as possible, oesign professionals understand that the strength of a warranty is nothing more than the strength of the product manufacturer, and that a four-page warranty probably has more exclusions than coverage. Additionally, the strength of the warranty is only as strong as the financial strength of the manufacturer, so accepting a 20-year roof warranty from a manufacturer that has only been in business for a year is probably going to be a problem if the owner has a claim in year 10.

Codes and Standards: There is a huge difference between these two. Codes are law, and the design professional has no choice but to abide by them. Reference standards are promulgated by trade organizations, firms like Underwriters Laboratories and others, and are incorporated into a project specification by reference. Using this approach means that quality can be ensured with very little effort. How much more work would it be to describe how Portland cement is manufactured versus stating that it must meet ASTM C150?

Too Many Product Decisions

As stated earlier, it has been said that the average building construction project requires 3,000 product decisions. Some of these are easy, while others are much more difficult, requiring extensive research and coordination. The design professional is constantly inundated with new products from multiple building product manufacturers, each of them trying to set themselves apart from the competition. How and when you approach the design professional can make the difference between success and failure.

Also understand that the product selection process is not always what it might seem. Sometimes it is 11:00 at night when the design professional is tired and wants to go home, but your website is poorly organized and lacking the information that he/she needs. What happens? They specify your competitor's product.

MARKETING MATERIALS

Hard Copy Versus Electronic

Hard copy is being replaced by electronic, but somewhat slowly, and senior office staff often prefer hard copy, while younger staff prefer electronic. At least for the foreseeable future, you will need at least some of your marketing materials in both formats.

Product Introductions

What we like to call your "pretty pictures" are absolutely essential for initial product consideration. These typically take the form of a brochure that introduces your products and lists basic attributes and advantages.

These product launches should be professionally prepared, either by an in-house marketing department or an outside consultant. Nothing stands out worse than a brochure designed by the company owner's amateurish young child. When looking for a marketing firm, find one that has experience in construction products, because a firm that sells washing detergent is not going to be sufficient for selling your product.

Design professionals are visual people, so say it with pictures, particularly on the cover. You can minimize the amount of reproductions with one well-designed project photograph that illustrates your product.

Even when all other product information goes electronic, there will always be a need for an effective hard-copy brochure. When you walk into a meeting with a design professional or meet one at a trade show, hand them your brochure.

Technical Literature

Once a design professional has decided to consider your product, he/she will need detailed technical information to be sure that your product will fill their needs.

Technical literature should be made available in either hard copy or electronic format as requested by the design professional.

Some of the information that they may need includes:

- **Product attributes**: What is your product and why should the design professional consider it? What are its advantages over competing products?
- **Uses and limitations**: Where should this product be used? And just as importantly, where should it not be used?
- **Tests and certifications**: Has the product been tested to industry standards? Does it meet building code requirements? Does it have third-party certifications for sustainability or other required attributes?
- **Installation**: How and by whom will the product be installed? Does it require a factory-trained or certified installer?
- **Maintenance**: Can the product be maintained by the owner's maintenance personnel, or is specialized training required? Are special tools needed?
- **Availability**: Is the product available nationally or only regionally? design professionals do not want to specify products that may not be available at the project locale. Is it available only through authorized distributors?

- **Sustainability**: Does the product contain recycled content? Is it considered a regional or local product? Is it a low-VOC product?

Drawing Details

In order to integrate products into their project, design professionals need drawing details so they can see how the object fits, for example, into a wall assembly along with other products.

Drawing details should be made available in either hard copy or electronic format as requested by the design professional.

Details should:

- Describe the product's installation and its relationship to other construction. Details in a different color or by shading may indicate elements not provided by your company.

- Be free from extraneous language and promotional language. Unnecessary declarations may be incorporated into the drawing files for a project and therefore become a contractual document. Furthermore, they cannot contain statements such as "by others," which means "not a part of this contract." Avoid marketing language designating your product as better than your competitor's.

- Be available in multiple Computer Aided Design (CAD) standards and be suitable for incorporation into Building Integrated Modeling (BIM) systems. While CAD has been the standard for design professionals for years, BIM is becoming the new standard. BIM is defined as the process of designing a building collaboratively using one coherent system of computer models rather than as separate sets of drawings. BIM is expensive and has a steep learning curve, but it will be the way that design professionals work in the future, and has already been adopted by most mid- and large-size firms.

- Be professionally prepared. Only those who have been trained in CAD and BIM systems understand what is needed for the correct input and use of information in these systems, hence, find someone who is qualified.

- ✦ Be free from copyrights. You don't want your competitors acquiring your details, but why would you want to keep design professionals from using them?

Guide Specifications

Guide specifications are specification section "templates" containing editing notes to assist design professionals in product selection and specifying. They are prepared according to CSI/CSC principles so that they can be incorporated into a project manual, along with the many other sections needed to complete a project.

For guide specifications, electronic versions are a must, while hard copy is optional.

Guide specifications should be:

- ✦ Based on your product without attempting to close the specification, since closed specifications are rarely allowed. Closed specifications are accomplished in one of two ways: by stating the product substitutions are not allowed or by writing the specification in such a way that no other products meet the specified requirements. The first case is easy for the design professional to find and correct, while the latter can be very difficult.

- ✦ Free from promotional language. Since these specifications will be edited to suit a particular project and incorporated into a project manual, they will become part of a construction contract and, as such, must be free of marketing language.

- ✦ Available in word processor format. Most design professionals work in either Word or WordPerfect, so a PDF file is of little use to them. They need to be able to edit the specification to suit their project requirements.

- ✦ Professionally prepared. Find an experienced specification consultant to prepare these. Even an architect may not have sufficient experience to correctly set the files up to lead the user through the many product decisions that must be made, particularly on complex products.
- ✦ Free from copyrights. Just like drawing details, design professionals need to be able to incorporate these into their projects.

Product Binders

An office library binder is a convenient way to offer all product information in a single location. It can include a product brochure, technical data, tests and certifications, a guide specification, and even samples (if small and lightweight).

Office libraries are being phased out due to the availability of electronic data but are still viable in many firms. Ask before you leave an office library file with a design professional, as your $50 binder could end up in the recycling bin if not requested.

Consider the following when designing your product binder:

- ✦ Utilize 3-ring format to allow for updating.
- ✦ Identify with the CSI/CSC Division number, e.g., 04, 05, etc. on the spine. This is how design professionals file the binders.
- ✦ Include your business card or a contact page, and a sticker or page inside with space to note updates.

Samples

With design professionals, "show and tell" really works, because design professionals are visual people. Passing samples around during a product presentation is an effective way to get them interested. Don't be upset if they poke, scratch, or break your sample; they are simply testing its physical attributes.

Don't overwhelm the design professional, as space in their libraries is limited. Ask if the design professional wants samples now, or allow them to call when they need them.

EFFECTIVE TECHNICAL ASSISTANCE

Reaching Design Professionals

Effectively reaching out to design professionals can be a time-consuming and frustrating process, depending on how much time and budget your company has, but there are time-proven ways to reach them.

Lunch-and-Learns

Most design professionals now need continuing education credits in order to retain their professional licenses, so lunch-and-learns are a nearly foolproof way to enter their doors. These are now so popular that if you contact a design professional and offer to schedule a course, you may be standing in line or waiting for a cancellation.

The easy way to get in the architect's office is to offer a one-hour face-to-face course. Members of the American Institute of Architects (AIA) must earn 18 LUs (learning units) from registered AIA/CES providers each year, and 12 of those must be in the topic areas of health, safety, and welfare (HSW). Architects also must complete continuing education requirements to renew most state licenses. There are more than 3,000 continuing education providers with a catalog of more than 75,000 approved courses. You can also contact your local AIA chapter to provide your course at their meetings. Develop an interesting course, or have an experienced company do the work for you.

Also, architectural firms are now increasingly asking for LEED 4.0 documentation, specifically a Health Product Declaration (HPD), be submitted before a lunch-and-learn can be scheduled. Companies such as Elixir Environmental (www.elixirenvironmental.com) can assist you with developing the required HPD chemical transparency document.

For credits through the American Institute of Architects' (AIA) CE program, presentations must be non-proprietary, with only the first and last slide showing your company name. Everything in between has to educate the architect without naming products. Some building product representatives are hesitant to do this, but it actually works to their advantage. What better way to show that you are the expert in your field than by talking to a group of architects about why they should select metal widgets over plastic ones?

The U.S. Green Building Council (USGBC) also has continuing education requirements for its approximately 200,000 members. All registered LEED professionals are required to maintain their qualification by earning continuing education hours. LEED Green Associates must earn 15 continuing education hours within two years of earning their credential. LEED accredited professionals must earn 30 continuing education hours within two years of earning their credential.

Companies such as GreenCE, Inc. (www.GreenCE.com) can develop and host your sustainable online course and make it available to design professionals 24/7. They can also report credits to AIA and USGBC/GBCI and email the participants a certificate of completion when passing the online test. Let them do all the administrative work so you can spend your time marketing.

Seminars
Seminars are becoming one of the best ways to reach the design professional, especially all-day events where the design professional can

receive up to eight hours of AIA or USGBC/GBCI credits. Typically, the sponsor of the event asks eight speakers to provide their one-hour AIA presentation to a room full of design professionals. Many times, the event can also be registered with USGBC/GBCI for continuing education credit for LEED professionals. The design professionals like this event because they can receive 8 hours of CE credit while taking only one day off work! Plus, they can meet after the presentation with the speaker about his/her products and possibly specify one of their projects. One successful event company to contact to get on their speaker list is the CE Academy, Inc. (www.CEAcademyinc.com).

Blogs

Blogs are a great way to market your product technology and build relationships with those who can specify the products. Sharing information can teach design professionals about the benefits of the products and what the applications are. You have substantial knowledge stored away in your brain that the architect needs to know, so educate them. You will become the go-to subject-matter expert, grow a professional network, and connect with potential specification writers who come to you for advice. A great blog example is www.greence.com/spec-shaman.

Know how to talk about LEED (www.USGBC.org).

LEED changes the way we think about how buildings and communities are planned, constructed, maintained, and operated. Leaders around the world have made LEED the most widely used third-party verification for green buildings, with around 2.2 million square feet certified daily.

There are approximately 200,000 LEED professionals, and many calls made to architects will involve a LEED professional. Know their language by studying the terminology. Learn what Material and Resources credits projects can achieve by using your products. These credits can be summarized on "GreenDocs," which architects will ask you for when working on sustainable projects. A source to help write this technical documentation for LEED professionals is www.GreenCE.com.

There is a free course on LEED for manufacturers to review, and there also is a study guide for the LEED exams at www.greence.com/freeleedexamprep.

Webinars

With internet technology, it is possible to get connected with architects across the globe at any time we want. A web-based seminar or webinar is a presentation of your product or technology conducted over the internet using video conferencing software. The host uses conferencing equipment and multimedia to connect to viewers or listeners interactively, including voice communications, live or prerecorded videos, online presentations, product demonstrations, text chats and more. These are usually your AIA or USGBC courses for continuing education credit. You are the presenter, and whatever is on your computer screen, usually a PowerPoint presentation, is shown to your attendees. You use a microphone and the audience can hear you or call in by telephone. The best time for webinars is usually at lunchtime so design professionals can watch during lunch.

Office Visits

A direct presentation to decision makers remains one of the most effective ways to market your product. The interaction between design professional and building product representative allows for the exchange of ideas and answering of questions.

There are three types of office visits:

- ✦ **Introductory**: Let's say that you have just visited with a design professional when you realize there is a similar office across the street. Without an appointment, don't expect to spend much time with them; spend 5 minutes and use it as an information-gathering visit. Find out the size of the office and what type of projects they work on. You might briefly review one product per visit, but no more. Inquire about a convenient time to schedule a longer presentation.

- **Product Specific**: Make an appointment. Spend 30 minutes; 60 minutes for AIA-accredited presentation (usually a lunch-and-learn). This is a direct presentation to a specific individual or individuals. Present one product line in depth per visit. Provide literature, guide specifications, and samples. Providing a box lunch seminar will cover all office personnel.

- **Specification**: This is a presentation for decision makers with a specific product for a specific project at the proper time. Specification presentations are generally in response to the design professional's request to consult on a specific project. Spend adequate time to fulfill their needs! Do not schedule these as back-to-back meetings, as you have no control over how long they will last. Be the expert: Know your product, your industry, and building-code requirements.

Trade Shows

Organizations such as the American Institute of Architects (AIA), Construction Specifications Institute (CSI), U.S. Green Building Council (USGBC), and others hold annual trade shows that can be of great benefit to building product manufacturers, if approached properly.

Pre-Planning

- Establish specific event objectives, e.g., "generate leads" or "advance image with design professionals."

- Understand the audience, as every show is different. They can be design professionals only, mixed, or trade only.

- Use pre-show "hooks" such as marketing through the show organizer. Give a compelling reason to stop by your booth.

- Stack your team: Select carefully to ensure the right mix. Assign outgoing personalities to greeting, but have experts available to answer in-depth technical questions. Take only individuals who are enthusiastic about your products, and have two staff in attendance at all times. Do refresher training.

Show Logistics
- ✦ Assign specific show-hour duties, including greeter, lead management, and technical assistance.
- ✦ Arrange for after-exhibit happy hours, parties, dinners, and special events; reach your audience with less cost, yet impress them.
- ✦ Check out your competition. How does their booth compare to yours, both in appearance and number of attendees present? What do they do to engage attendees?

Booth Space Selection: Get in early for the widest selection. Look for opportunities to stand out.

Your Booth Space
- ✦ Self-contained "pop up" booths work well for large spaces, while pull-up "banners" and a table can work for small spaces.
- ✦ Say it with graphics: Design professionals are visual people, lured to strong design and powerful graphics.
- ✦ Keep it simple: Attendees should know what you do in one simple glance; too much text to read and comprehend makes them walk away.
- ✦ Consider live demonstrations: Many products lend themselves to live demonstrations, but keep them short.

Staff Conduct
- ✦ **Attire**: Appropriate to the occasion, which is usually business casual. Color-matched shirts displaying your company logo create a unified effect and identify booth staff to design professionals.
- ✦ **Attitude and Approach**: Make eye contact, say good morning/afternoon. Be outgoing but not aggressive; avoid being a huckster. Offer to solve or help with a problem.

Bad Booth Habits

- **Eating**: Nobody wants to interrupt a meal nor does the smell of corn chips and chili pie really help your cause. Avoid cups, bottles, and trash in your booth.
- **Sitting down**: Standing up shows your interest in attendees. If you do sit down during slow periods, stand up immediately when someone approaches.
- **Texting/Talking on phone**: This shows a lack of interest in the show and attendees.

Following Up After the Show

- **The importance of follow-up**: Many design professionals come away from product shows with thoughts of how to incorporate what they have seen into current and future projects. Even if they do not have a current need, failure to follow up can be viewed as being non-supportive.
- **Evaluate your success**: Did you meet your objectives? What about your budget? What changes do you want to make for the next show or next year?

Publications

Periodicals, such as *Architecture, Architectural Record*, and *The Specifier*, accept advertising, but the costs can be extremely high, and circulation is down from its peak 10 or 20 years ago. Most design professionals get their product news online now.

The Internet

When properly approached, the internet is one of your best marketing opportunities. Design professionals approach product searches in different ways, and you need to consider using all of them:

- **Construction product directories**: These are websites where building product manufacturers place their products for a fee, allowing design professionals to access them for free. They can range from simple one-page ads to full offerings of product selectors, technical data, guide specifications, and CAD or BIM files.

- **Cloud-based collaborative websites**: This technology is the newest entry of this market. These websites offer the ability to access master specification systems, integrate with BIM systems, and collaborate with other project team members.
- **Manufacturer websites**: With the huge advances in search engines, it is now easy to find products on specific manufacturer's websites rather than using another method. Searching for "widgets" brings up a multitude of product options that can be easily accessed.

When designing company websites, keep the following in mind:

- Do not assume that the design professional knows which product is needed before they get to your website. Many websites for construction products require the design professional to select either a product number or name from a lengthy list, while all they may know is that they want a latex paint and not a stain. Offer them a generic list of products to choose from first, then let them drill down to the exact product.
- Do not make design professionals register as a prerequisite to your website access or offer an "opt out" button. It is common information that you just want to gain information on potential products. But when it is 11:00 at night, and the design professional just needs your guide specification before finishing that project, filling out a form that asks for their annual salary is just an insult. Don't be surprised if upon checking the forms from the previous day you get answers like "Name: Yes."
- Poorly prepared websites stand out from the rest, and not for good reason. A reasonable investment here will reap rewards as design professionals find your website. Have your website professionally prepared.

✦ **Provide separate pages for design professionals, constructors and homeowners:** If you sell to multiple market segments, break them out separately. If you sell paints and related products, don't make the design professional slog through paintbrushes and drop cloths to find the solid's content of your latex paint.

Assistance During Various Project Phases
Schematic Design
Assistance to the design professional during this phase will be limited primarily to discussions concerning primary exterior and interior building components and the furnishing of samples for preliminary color selections. Gather information about the project and be ready for more detailed assistance during the next phase.

Design Development
Assistance during this phase will be similar to SD for major exterior and interior components, but will expand to include other components as well, such as floor finishes for critical interior spaces. Be prepared to discuss product costs, details, and specifications in a preliminary manner.

Contract Documents
Since all product decisions will have been made by the end of this phase, assistance to the design professional will reach its peak. Costs, details, and specifications will be finalized, and you may be asked to assist in any or all of these efforts.

Bidding/Negotiations
Since the only documents issued by the design professional during this phase are addenda, assistance will be primarily limited to answering requests by the design professional for information related to product substitutions.

Contract Administration
Refer to Construction Submittals (p. 77) for a list of documents that may need to be produced during this phase. Each project specification

section contains specific information related to the submittals required for a specific project.

Finding Project Leads

Most likely the best method for identifying potential projects is via your personal relationships with design professionals, so just ask. If the design professional has been working with you in developing a project, they will typically want you involved during construction – just one of the many benefits of becoming the design professional's expert.

Document services can also be a source for project leads. Services such as Dodge Reports, CMD Group, BidClerk, iSqFt, and others provide these services for a fee. The extent of the reporting depends on what you subscribe to, and the information can range from modest to overwhelming. There are several things to keep in mind when using these services:

- **Timeliness of data**: Projects listed under headings like "Four new schools, Dallas Independent School District" often mean that a reporter picked up the information from a newspaper after a bond election was passed. These projects may not hit the streets for years. Conversely, a project that is out for bids will result in "reactionary selling," and the specifications have already been written; therefore, you will be chasing the design professional to add your name.
- **Look for trends**: Rather than chasing after individual projects, look for design professionals who steadily work on the types of projects that you pursue, then acquire them.

Getting in the Door

Too often the building product representative will find that approaching design professionals is a time-consuming, frustrating process. This is primarily due to the fact that they do not understand design professionals, project phases, or the product selection process. Let's look at a few basic problems:

- **Too early in the project schedule**: Most product decisions are made later in the design process than most people want to believe. Early stages of a project are dedicated to initial design where product selection is not a consideration. What do you do when you call on the design professional too early? Ask when it would be appropriate to come back.

- **Too late in the project schedule**: Once product decisions are made and incorporated into drawings and specifications, those decisions become difficult or impossible to modify. At this point, you are doing what we call "reactionary selling," which is calling up the design professional and saying, "Me, too – I have one of those. Please add me to your specifications."

- **Too often**: Don't be a pest! Projects progress at a predictable rate, so calling on the design professional every two weeks will not endear you to them.

- **The gatekeeper**: Most mid- and large-size offices have a receptionist whom you will need to get past in order to get to the person or persons making product decisions. They may also be responsible for scheduling "lunch-and-learns" for the office. This person can be your friend or your enemy, depending on how you approach them. Be pleasant, be respectful, and don't forget to invite them when you do show up for that "lunch-and-learn," because the cost of one boxed lunch can make you an instant ally.

- **What happened?** Let's say that you did everything right while working with the design professional, providing technical assistance and getting an assurance that your product will be used on the project. Then the project is issued with another product specified. Don't hold it against the design professional; it could be pressure from the owner or changing program requirements that resulted in the change of products. Keep your cool and you will have another chance.

Getting the Specification

Even after all of their hard work, many building product representatives will fail to close the deal because they do not "get the specification." Doing everything correctly with the design professional, calling on them at the right time, getting them the information they need, and assisting them in developing drawings and specifications are necessary endeavors, but follow-through is crucial.

"Getting the specification" is nothing more than getting the design professional to either write a project specification around their product or add them to a list of approved manufacturers/products contained in a project specification.

After the Specification

Even when you do "get the specification," your work is not done. You must follow up with constructors and suppliers to ensure that your product is included in the bidding/pricing process before a construction contract is assigned, and you must be prepared to defend the specification against product substitutions.

A product substitution is a request by a constructor, subcontractor, or supplier to use a product different from the specified product. The most common reason for product substitutions is to use a product of lower cost, but other factors may come into play as well. Design professionals usually review product substitution requests, and many publish a form specifically for this purpose that must be used.

Product substitutions are a fact of life, so be ready to defend the use of your product. Just as you would when presenting your product to a design professional, be prepared to make the same presentation to a constructor, subcontractor, or supplier. When they hit you with your competitor's lower cost, show them how your product excels with fewer failures, callbacks, and jobsite meetings with design professionals and owners. Most people will be convinced to spend a bit more upfront if their downside risk is reduced or eliminated.

Construction Submittals

Design professionals utilize a group of submittals from the constructor to ensure that the required products are correctly incorporated into the work:

Review Submittals

Design professionals review and approve or reject these submittals, which are prepared specifically for each project.

- ✦ **Shop Drawings**: These are drawings, diagrams, schedules, and other data prepared to show some portion of the work. They can be standard details but may also need to be prepared to illustrate the unique aspects of each project.

- ✦ **Product Data**: These are defined as illustration, standard schedules, performance charts, instructions, diagrams, and other information to illustrate materials or equipment for some portion of the work. Information that is applicable to the specific project should be highlighted, and non-applicable information should be marked through.

- ✦ **Samples**: These are physical examples that illustrate materials, equipment, or workmanship and establish standards by which the work will be judged. When the product contains a range of colors or patterns, such as for natural stone, samples need to illustrate the full range that the design professional can expect to see on the project.

Quality Control Submittals

Design professionals request test reports, certifications, and other documents to establish compliance with the specifications that they have prepared. These submittals are often forwarded to the owner for their records, and can be used if a problem surfaces after occupancy of the project.

Post Construction Submittals

These submittals are for the owner's benefit during occupancy and use of the facility.

- **Project Record Documents**: These documents consist of drawings and specifications marked up to show any variations and changes made during construction, including the substitution of products from those originally specified.
- **Warranties**: Extended warranties, beyond the typical one-year general warranty issued by the constructor, are issued by product manufacturers for components such as roofing and mechanical systems.

MAKING EFFECTIVE PRODUCT PRESENTATIONS

Getting your building products specified by architects isn't rocket science, but it takes persistence and patience. First, you need a great building product. If your product is a cheap piece of junk, ridden with design deficiencies, made from toxic substances like mercury and asbestos, and assembled by underage children in some third-world country ruled by a ruthless dictator, then you might want to rethink your plan. However, if you manufacture a great product, there are significant steps you can take to improve your chances of product specification.

Manufacturers who create products that eliminate problems for architects will form strong, positive associations with designers over time. It can take months or even years for architects to embrace a product. Most architects are not willing to be a guinea pig for a new product. Typically, architects like a time-proven product from a reputable manufacturer. Products need to deliver on their promises. Taking into consideration a design professional's motivation and ability to specify a given product, and adding a trigger, can help building product manufacturers increase product specifications. Delivering effective product presentations to design professionals is essential for success. Let's review 10 recommendations for product reps.

1. **Establish an objective for the presentation.** Why did you walk into the design professional's office? Is this an introductory call, or are you trying to get a specification on a particular project? Do not confuse your efforts.

2. **Make the presentation clear and understandable.** Many building product representatives talk over the heads of their audience, thinking that this architect knows every screw in every aluminum window assembly. Another problem is that representatives talk in acronyms. While a cantilever might make perfect sense to you, it means nothing to a design professional.

3. **Make the presentation personal and flexible.** Nobody likes a canned presentation. Turning on a PowerPoint presentation to autopilot while you stand at the back of the room is the fastest way to lose your audience. Hence, many a building product representative has lost out on a specification because, when the design professional asked a question, they just nodded and went right back to their canned presentation.

4. **Make the presentation participatory.** Get people involved and ask questions. Do they use these types of windows? Do they ever have problems with them? Most people want a chance to tell their stories, not just listen to yours.

5. **Let the design professional steer the agenda.** You may never get back to your agenda, and that is great. The design professional is testing you to see if they want you on their team. Plus, you can always ask to come back for a follow-up meeting.

6. **Gather information.** As much as you are trying to sell your product, you are also there to gather information. How big is this firm? What type of projects do they work on? Do they ever specify aluminum widgets over steel ones?

7. **Avoid negative selling.** One of the worst things that you can do as a building product representative is to run down your competition. When you ask a design professional whose widgets they specify and they say "Acme," how do you know that the Acme representative is not his/her brother, and you just asked if they were still specifying that junk? You can actually negatively sell, if you do it carefully. "Acme Widgets? Good product. We believe that ours is better because…" and then explain why.

8. **Dress appropriately.** Some firms allow very lax dress codes while others require much higher ones. In general, dress codes have relaxed quite a bit over the past 20 years, but you should still take pride in your appearance. At least on the first visit, men should wear slacks and a dress shirt, and women a similar professional outfit. If the office is pretty relaxed, you can always dress down a bit next time.

9. **Be respectful of time.** If you set up the meeting for an hour, then take an hour, and no more. You can always state that you have used your allotted time, and that you can continue if the design professional desires, or you can schedule a second meeting. Run over the allotted time without asking and you will not be asked back.

10. **Close with questions.** What is a good question to ask a design professional? "Can you add my product to this project's specifications?" Better? "Can you add my product to your office master specification?"

In addition, let's review three typical product rep office visits.

- ✦ **Introductory:** Let's say that you've just visited a design professional when you realize that there is another architect across the street. Without an appointment, don't expect to spend much time with them; spend 5 minutes and use it as an information-gathering call. Find out the size of the office and what type of projects they work on. If you're lucky, you might briefly review one product per visit, but no more. Ask when a good time would be to schedule a longer presentation.

- **Product Specific:** Make an appointment. Spend 30 minutes on average or 60 minutes for an AIA-accredited presentation (usually a lunch-and-learn). This is a direct presentation to a specific individual or individuals. Present one product line in depth per visit, as well as furnish literature, guide specifications and samples, providing a box-lunch seminar covers all office personnel with one visit.

- **Specification:** This is a presentation for decision makers with a specific product for a specific project at the proper time, usually in response to the design professional's request to consult on a specific project. Spend adequate time to satisfy their needs; however, do not schedule these back to back, as you have no control over how long they will last. Be the expert; know your product, your industry, and building code requirements.

Providing Assistance During Various Project Phases

Product reps will be required to provide assistance to the architect, specifier, interior designer, contractor, etc. throughout the various project phases. Let's review the various project phases and the correct course of action.

- **Schematic Design:** Assistance to the design professional during this phase will be limited primarily to discussions concerning primary exterior and interior building components and the furnishing of samples for preliminary color selections. Gather information about the project and be ready for more detailed assistance during the next phase.

- **Design Development:** Assistance during this phase will be similar to SD for major exterior and interior components, but will expand to include other components as well, such as floor finishes for critical interior spaces. Be prepared to discuss product costs, details, and specifications in a preliminary manner.

- **Contract Documents:** Since all product decisions will have been made by the end of this phase, assistance to the design professional will reach its peak. Costs, details, and specifications will be finalized, and you may be asked to assist in any or all of these efforts.

- **Bidding/Negotiations:** Since the only documents issued by the design professional during this phase are addenda, assistance will primarily be limited to answering requests by the design professional for information related to product substitutions.

- **Contract Administration:** Refer to the Construction Submittals section below for a list of documents that may need to be produced during this phase. Each project specification section contains specific information related to the submittals required for a specific project.

Additional Assistance

The design professional requires product information to create drawings and specifications. Product representatives educate and advise the architect to get the product specified correctly during their office visits.

Thousands of products are incorporated into every project. Product costs may be affected by information such as lead times, special field testing, customized orders, or inspections, and should be brought to the architect's attention in a timely manner. Reps must have this information readily available.

In addition to assisting the architect with product decisions, product representatives can add value to consulting in other ways. These include providing product guide specifications, cost estimate information, on-site storage recommendations, reference standards, and making the architect aware of code requirements.

Product reps can also assist with the project drawings, which likewise require technical assistance in order to verify proper use of the product, ensure accurate incorporation of the correct product in the project, and verify that special conditions are addressed correctly.

Product representatives can provide technical assistance in drawing development in the following ways:

- ✦ Establish specific material locations and dimensions
- ✦ Verify that products meet local code requirements
- ✦ Assist in detailing the product interface with adjacent building materials
- ✦ Provide manufacturer's standard drawings or BIM files for proper product application

The product information provided during the office visit may contain standard drawing details and product guide specifications, and the product representative may ask to review the drawings for a design professional on a project in the construction documents (CD) stage. This will help the architect become more comfortable with the level of service that can be expected by the rep. This type of technical assistance builds the design professional's confidence in the product representative and ensures that the proper product information is being submitted.

Product reps can also make the design professional aware of any continuing education opportunities available in various formats. The rep can offer to provide a lunch-and-learn at the office, usually an AIA, USGBC/GBCI, IDCEC or RCEP registered course. architects get a generic education on the manufacturer's technology and receive a certificate of completion. The education counts for the AIA or other association's CE requirements or for state registration requirements. Online courses, webinars, and seminar educational events can be discussed.

10 MISTAKES MADE BY PRODUCT PRESENTERS

1. **No presentation objectives.** Walking into a design professional's office without knowing why you are there can be disastrous. Some building product representatives are simply following their boss' instructions to make 10 sales calls this week, but is that really the objective? Think through what your approach is and offer the design professional some real benefit for spending time with you.

2. **Mediocre first impression.** It is never more true that you never get a second chance to make a good first impression than with design professionals. Their time is limited, and they will remember if you wasted it.

3. **Lack of preparation.** You might not be asked for the certified test results for your product for a year, but having to run to your car and retrieve it is pretty bad. Anticipate everything that you might need, and have it ready.

4. **Poor visual aids.** Nothing is worse than placing your sample product on the design professional's conference table and having it fall apart. No matter how much you try to explain that your

lockset really does hold up well, they will never specify it. Inspect samples regularly, and tighten or replace when necessary.

5. **Lack of enthusiasm.** If you are not excited about your product, how can you expect the design professional to be? You might be selling concrete aggregates, so promote your product with zeal to bolster the belief that they are the best ones available.

6. **Weak eye contact.** This is especially true when talking to larger groups. Make eye contact with everyone in the room; it makes them feel included.

7. **No audience involvement.** Droning on about your product for an hour is a surefire way to lose your audience. Ask questions, and get them to talk about their experiences.

8. **Lack of facial expression.** Just like weak eye contact, this shows a lack of enthusiasm about your product. Be motivated and express it with your body language.

9. **Sticky floor syndrome.** When talking to a larger group, move around the room. Not only does it keep people from falling asleep, but it keeps them from texting, as well.

10. **Ineffective closing.** What is the best closing? By closing with the question, "What projects are you working on?" is good; even better is asking the design professional to add you to their office master specification. This is a solid way to ensure that while you are out golfing, they are writing specifications on your product.

OFFICE VISIT 'MUSTS'

1. **Have all necessary product information on hand.** Never leave those test results in your car. By the time you have retrieved them, the design professional will have taken a phone call, and you have lost your chance.

2. **Be thoroughly familiar with your product.** Do not waste your time calling on design professionals until you comprehend your product inside and out. Yes, there will be times when you cannot answer a question, but promise the design professional an answer, and then make sure to follow up.

3. **Be ready to compare your product to your competition.** An open and honest discussion helps the design professional to know who you consider to be your worthy competition. Remember, they are rarely allowed to write closed specifications.

4. **Admit your product's limitations.** Don't lose sight of your long-term goal of being the design professional's expert by selling out for short-term profits. Product disasters linger long in the mind of the design professional.

5. **Recognize that many specifications cannot be closed to your product.** Remember that there are very few cases when a design professional can write a closed specification. Enjoy the ones that are closed, but be ready to compete head-to-head when the challenge arises.

6. **Recognize that results are often not immediate.** It might be years before you see a specification on your product from a design professional. Slow and steady wins this race.

7. **Respond promptly to the design professional's request for additional information.** You might think that the design professional is just sending you on a wild goose chase, and you could be right, but imagine their surprise and respect when you actually follow up.

EDUCATION EQUALS SPECIFICATION

How do architects, specifiers, and contractors perceive your products? What if these business professionals' perceptions are wrong? Does it matter? Marketing is not a battle of products, it's a battle of perceptions. An effective education campaign can be a major tool in creating positive perceptions.

It is difficult to change an architect's mind. Marketing delivered to architects and specifiers may slowly build a favorable opinion over time about your products, but once perception about a building product is envisioned, it can be tough to change. The best building product doesn't always get specified. Continuing education courses can teach architects about a building product's benefits; however, that's not the end of the marketing game. The world of marketing consists of illusions. While perception of a building product is the reality, everything else is a delusion.

Secondhand opinions can have a major effect on a manufacturer's building products. If an architect's friend specified the curtain wall system on a project that failed and led to water infiltration issues, then spread secondhand awareness may affect future specifications. Secondhand perceptions can result in the "everybody knows" principle, where architects favor or despise products based on other's perceptions.

Continuing education (CE) programs are the most effective tools for building product manufacturers to reach architects, specifiers, interior designers, contractors, LEED consultants, and many other design professionals. We will explore the benefits of continuing education and the various delivery methods manufacturers can use.

Brand Awareness

How can building product manufacturers increase brand awareness? Brand awareness is the extent to which your product is recognized by architects, specifiers, contractors, and other design professionals. Brand awareness should be one of the first steps performed by product manufacturers, as it affects the specification opportunities that are made when it comes to the product selection phase. Out of sight equates to out of mind. Moreover, if a designer has no familiarity with your brand, they are less likely to specify your product.

In the old days, building product manufacturers utilized everything from newspapers to radio ads to promote their brand. Those forms of media are outdated for increasing brand awareness for most commercial building products. Magazines are still being utilized by some building product manufacturers to spread the word about their products. However, as magazine subscriptions dwindle and ad rates increase, manufacturers are looking for more modern and effective solutions for brand advertisement and product recognition. The internet has spawned an entire ecosystem of tools for building product manufacturers to use.

One of the most effective and economical ways to build brand and product awareness is through education. **Education equals specifications.** If an architect does not know about your product and its benefits, how the heck can they specify it? CE courses help design professionals maintain their mandatory CE hours while learning about your product. Education is a no-brainer for companies that want to teach architects about their products' benefits and increase their brand awareness.

Nearly every state in the country requires continuing education for architects. If architects fail to meet their mandatory CE requirements, they can lose their license to practice architecture! In addition, several professional organizations require their members to take CE courses annually. The American Institute of Architects (AIA), U.S. Green Building Council (USGBC), and other professional organizations require their members to maintain their credentials through CE courses.

AIA Continuing Education

AIA continuing education is required for AIA members to maintain their professional membership. There are more than 90,000 AIA members required to complete 18 Learning Units (LU) annually for membership renewal. Each LU counts as one hour of continuing education. AIA education provides a significant opportunity for building product manufacturers to reach the top decision makers and educate them about their products.

An AIA CE course must be at least one (1) hour in length and consist of a direct learning activity for a minimum of 60 minutes. The course can consist of 50 minutes of presentation time, followed by 10 minutes of a question-and-answer session directly related to course content. A building product manufacturer's course content must be unbiased, non-promotional, and generic. The course should be created by a qualified subject matter expert and presented by individuals with a background on the subject matter.

Before you start developing your AIA online education course, you better ask yourself one question: "Am I the most qualified person to write this course?" You don't need to be William Shakespeare, but you better be knowledgeable about your topic and be a proficient storyteller. Every AIA online course should be written by a subject matter expert who can convey the crucial aspects of a building product while keeping the audience entertained. How many snooze-fest PowerPoint presentations have you experienced? The subject matter expert should be very familiar with the topic, the industry terminology, and provide anecdotal content when possible. Audiences love case studies and real-life examples.

USGBC Education

LEED v4 was launched in November 2013. Yet, many building product manufacturers are still unprepared in today's marketplace. Despite several new opportunities, many building product manufacturers haven't developed Health Product Declarations (HPDs) for LEED v4. Other companies have failed to update their LEED product documentation from LEED v3 to LEED v4. Forward-thinking manufacturers and early adopters will reap the benefits of LEED v4 while others will be playing catch-up and have fewer specification opportunities.

Building product manufacturers can increase opportunities for getting specified on LEED-certified projects through education. As of 2017, there are more than 200,000 LEED professionals. Architects, engineers, interior designers, contractors, and other design professionals who maintain a LEED credential need continuing education. LEED courses provide a significant avenue for manufacturers to educate LEED Accredited Professionals (AP) about their products.

As of 2017, there are more than 90,500 commercial projects that are LEED certified with more than 5.8 billion certified commercial square feet. LEED is not going away, and any manufacturer who thinks LEED is a fad is misinformed. So, how can building product manufacturers leverage LEED v4 to get specified? Developing a GBCI general hour course or LEED-specific hour course can help reach thousands of LEED APs who need their mandated CE hours. LEED APs must earn 30 continuing education hours to maintain their credential. At least 6 hours must be LEED-specific hours related to their LEED specialty. The remaining 24 hours can all be general CE hours. Once again, this is a significant opportunity for manufacturers to educate thousands of architects about their products.

Continuing Education Delivery Formats

Building product manufacturers need to invest their marketing dollars wisely. Manufacturers with limited budgets and a small staff need to ensure that they get the best return on their investment. Developing a CE course can be an expensive endeavor for some manufacturers, especially when they invest in strategies with low or zero ROI (return on investment). Avoiding certain pitfalls and maximizing investment is crucial. There are three primary delivery formats for CE courses: online, webinar, and face-to-face. Each delivery format has pros and cons and should be evaluated to meet a manufacturer's specific requirements. We will explore each delivery format and how they can assist in product specification.

Online CE Course Format

An online CE course is one of the most effective tools a manufacturer can use to increase product specifications. Online CE courses educate architects, specifiers, interior designers, engineers, contractors, LEED consultants, and other decision makers in a format that is convenient, easy to use, and extremely effective. Online CE courses can educate design professionals 24 hours a day, during the week, weekends, and holidays. It's a little-known industry secret that design professionals often obtain their mandatory CE hours on weekends, late at night, and even during the holidays. Architects are often slammed at the office and cannot spare billable hours during the day to take a class. Online CE courses solve a major time-crunch problem for architects and provide an amazing opportunity for manufacturers. The benefits for product manufacturers include:

- ✦ Educate architects and decision makers about your products 24 hours a day, 365 days a year!
- ✦ Generate leads by collecting course user information and follow up with potential customers
- ✦ Build brand awareness and increase SEO opportunities

- Save time and money by reducing product reps' journeys to make face-to-face presentations nationwide

Although there are a handful of product manufacturers who host their own online CE programs, most companies opt to work with an existing platform provider. Typically, a platform provider is an education provider with the AIA, USGBC, IDCEC, and other important credentialed organizations. Platform providers already have a learning management system in place for users to take courses, quizzes, and to issue certificates to users for their mandatory CE hours. In addition, platform providers can drive a significant amount of traffic to their hosted courses. Most architects don't want to visit several dozen websites to obtain their CE hours. They prefer to visit one website to learn about multiple products. Platform providers save manufacturers money, time, and precious resources.

Microsoft PowerPoint has been the primary tool for developing CE courses for decades now. It has been the warhorse of tools but also the butt of many jokes. Death by PowerPoint is a nightmare no one wants to suffer. We've all endured bad PowerPoint presentations where the speaker reads the slides verbatim, mountains of bullet points drown out crummy stock photos and clip art, and architects suffer from narcolepsy and fall out of their chairs.

Microsoft's version of PowerPoint was officially launched on May 22, 1990, as a part of the Microsoft Office suite. It's more than a quarter century old and, in the wrong hands, can inflict damage to your brand and specification chances. However, PowerPoint can still be a powerful tool if used correctly. The best PowerPoint presentations utilize video, animation, and voice-over. Great PowerPoint presentations tell a story about a building product and aren't just lame sales pitches by overeager product reps looking to close the deal. PowerPoint presentations with voice-over work extremely well as online courses when exported as MPEG-4 files. These courses perform much better than all other formats except full video courses.

Online CE courses that use video have the highest participation rates in the industry. If you want architects to learn about your building products, there is no more effective method than video education. Video courses routinely outperform any other delivery format and justify their higher costs with better ROI. Architects want to learn about your building products, except in an engaging and entertaining way.

Cisco, the networking equipment manufacturer, released a significant study on video education. This groundbreaking research revealed several important benefits related to video education. Video allows architects to expand their understanding of complex subjects by strengthening the link between abstract ideas and practical applications. Video education also gives architects the opportunity to travel to remote locations to learn without ever leaving their office or home. Video is the ideal format for case studies, product installations, and education courses.

Research indicates that young professionals, such as architects and engineers, are fundamentally different from previous generations in the way they think and how they access, absorb, interpret, process, and use information. Today's design professionals are increasingly visual-spatial learners, able to multitask and interact with multimedia.

Video Course Case Study

The Copper Development Association Inc. (CDA) is the market development, engineering, and information services arm of the copper industry, chartered to enhance and expand markets for copper and its alloys in North America. The CDA represents the largest copper product manufacturers in the country that produce copper wall cladding, roofing, gutters, plumbing, electrical, and industrial products.

The CDA had a problem … How could they reach thousands of architects, specifiers, contractors, and other design professionals to promote their members' products and the benefits of copper? The CDA has a small marketing team and did not have the resources to travel and meet thousands of decision makers. How could the CDA increase copper product specifications, increase brand awareness, and maximize their ROI?

The CDA hired GreenCE, Inc., an education platform provider to develop a one-hour AIA and USGBC online education course to educate design professionals. The course is entitled *Oasis: Designing a LEED Campus in the Desert – Part 1*. The lesson focuses on the Health Sciences Education Building (HSEB) in Arizona, a $135 million medical school in downtown Phoenix, which is LEED certified. Over $2 million of copper cladding was utilized for the project. The online CE course provides architects with the opportunity to learn about the benefits of copper 24/7 and obtain their mandatory CE hours. The video-based course utilizes interviews, animation, and a building tour to create an educational and engaging experience.

The return-on-investment was significant for the CDA. The CDA's continuing education course is the best-performing online curriculum in the history of GreenCE, awarding more CE hours than any other AIA and USGBC course in the industry. Typical industry participation for online classes is 50 to 100 participants per month. The CDA's education course was launched in November 2012 and on average had 259 participants per month. The total number of participants for the course in year one was 3,109. Typically, CE lessons have a shelf life of 3 years. By the time the CDA course was in its fourth year of operation in 2016, it had awarded more than 7,658 AIA and GBCI credits since its launch.

The education program was such a success that the CDA developed a second video education course with GreenCE, and it was awarded 1,991 AIA and GBCI hours in its first year. The success of these programs can be attributed to a few significant factors. First, the course has broad appeal, because the video documents the design and construction of a fascinating medical school that includes engaging interviews with the entire project team. Second, the course received the much-sought-after

LEED-specific hour credit designation, which is very difficult to obtain. The GreenCE team of LEED Consultants, architects, and engineers created a course to meet these stringent standards. Finally, the course utilized 21st-century tools, such as high-definition video, animation, voice-over, and special effects to create an exciting story.

Webinar CE Course Format

Webinars are one of the most effective marketing tools a building product manufacturer can use. Webinars can offer more education benefits in one hour than any other sales and marketing program. How many other marketing programs do you know of that can educate 250 to 500 architects, specifiers, contractors, and engineers in one hour? Webinars should be an essential part of every manufacturer's marketing plan. Let's review how webinars can benefit product manufacturers:

- ✦ Educate 250 to 500 design professionals in one hour
- ✦ Generate leads by collecting participant data and engage in follow-up
- ✦ Save time and money by not traveling nationwide to educate hundreds of architects
- ✦ Create custom post-webinar survey to collect market and product data for your team
- ✦ Engage in a live Q&A session to talk directly to the architects about your products

To deliver a great webinar presentation, there are a few essential components to consider. What type of software and web-hosting platform are you going to use? How are you going to advertise and build participation for the event? Is the presentation going to be registered with the AIA and USGBC for continuing education hours? Finally, what is the topic and who is the presenter? You need a very engaging title and course description to entice people to sign up. Your presenter doesn't need to be a classically trained actor who enunciates every word like Daniel

Day-Lewis, but he or she better be able to speak clearly and articulate your message effectively.

Once again, partnering up with an education platform provider is a great way to maximize ROI. A platform provider will host, moderate, advertise, and issue CE hour certificates for users. In addition, a platform provider will register the course with the AIA, USGBC, IDCEC, and other professional organizations. Selecting the best platform provider is essential for a successful outcome.

Face-to-Face CE Course Format

Face-to-face education offers your product reps the opportunity to forge effective relationships with architects, specifiers, LEED professionals, engineers, and other design professionals. Your product reps can present their sponsored course at architecture firms across the country. The face-to-face course format, also known as a lunch-and-learn, is one of the most effective presentations for manufacturers. However, it is also the most expensive CE delivery format, since product reps must pay for travel (airfare, rental car, hotel, etc.), meals for architects, venue and equipment rental, and advertising.

Getting products specified can be difficult in a world of distractions, red tape, and limited time. Face-to-face education cuts through the clutter so that product reps can speak directly to the specifiers and project architects, and ensure that they understand their building products. Once again, partnering with an education platform provider can help significantly. CE Academy, Inc. is a company that coordinates live classroom events in 60 different cities across the country. They assist manufacturers in maximizing their ROI for face-to-face presentations.

Mistakes to Avoid When Developing a CE Course

If the primary delivery format for your AIA CE course is a Portable Document Format (PDF), then you're in trouble. The PDF was developed in the early 1990s to share documents, including text formatting and images, among users of different computer platforms. Using a PDF or Microsoft Word document as your primary delivery format is like reading a month-old newspaper to obtain information today instead of using the internet. Users typically download the PDF and read the document like a newspaper article. PDFs have their place in education, but should only be used as an additional resource (white paper, case study, etc.) and not as the primary format for your AIA or USGBC course.

Architects, spec writers, interior designers, and other professionals appreciate online CE courses that utilize 21st-century tools. Most PDF AIA education courses fail to garner much interest because they rely on pages saturated with heavy text and bullet points while offering few product images. Architects want to learn about a product by participating in a well-written and visually appealing course, not a 60-page PDF overflowing with mountains of text and bad clip art. PDFs also fail to take advantage of the best tools available, such as video clips and audio narration.

In addition, there are several limitations when using a PDF as a delivery format for AIA education. Older PDFs may use media embedded in them that is not playable on architects' devices. PDFs will not operate in many Apple iOS devices such as the iPad, which architects use to participate in education programs. The PDF is the equivalent of a printed page in machine reproducible form. It's one step up from a basic JPEG image. Interactivity and creativity is limited, which means there are fewer tools to use to educate architects about your products. Participation for PDF courses is abysmal. This is bad for your brand and results in poor ROI. Surprisingly, a major AEC education platform provider still uses this outdated delivery format as their primary educational tool. Invest your money where you get the highest return. Avoid developing online PDF courses at all costs!

Professional photography is essential for CE courses. Building product manufacturers can't afford to feature low-quality images in their presentation. How many presentations have been ruined by crummy images, poorly lit shots, and blurry snapshots? Your team may have written the greatest AIA presentation in history, but if the product photos are of poor quality, your endeavor was a waste of time and money.

Stock photography has its place in AIA presentations, but hiring a professional photographer or videographer can make a world of difference. Stock images are clichéd and can be used by everyone; therefore, the stock image you select may also end up in your competitor's presentation! Great photography sells more products. In side-by-side comparisons, most consumers choose brands with great photography over products with mediocre imagery.

Would you trust the janitor at your building to perform open-heart surgery on a patient? Then why would you let your forklift operator use an iPhone to shoot product presentation photos in your dimly lit factory? It's not logical! Nothing says "amateur" like a poorly lit photograph of a building product. Building product manufacturers want architects, specifiers, and contractors to trust them, and to trust that they run a professional shop. If your building product images are lousy, lack of excellence may indicate that your products or customer service are too.

Professional audiovisual services are highly recommended for installation tutorials, product demonstrations, case studies, and interviews. Video can take your online AIA course to the next level. Recordings give architects the opportunity to travel to remote locations to learn without ever leaving their classroom. Videos are uniquely suited for taking architects on "impossible" field trips, such as a tour inside a new net-zero LEED Platinum building project in New Zealand. Online CE courses that utilize video have the highest participation rates in the industry.

While shooting your kid's soccer game with your smartphone might be all right to show the family, that same approach won't work for shooting professional videos about your products. Just because your cousin

Jimmy bought a $500 video camera from Best Buy, that doesn't make him a globetrotting *National Geographic* photographer. Great photos and videos will help to create a great educational course. Investing in a professional photographer/videographer to capture your building products is a solid investment, because without professional images, your course is a waste of time and money.

Education Platform Providers

There are hundreds of AIA education providers. Most of them are building product manufacturers, industry associations, colleges, architecture firms, etc. However, there are fewer than a half-dozen educational platform providers that cater to the needs of product manufacturers. When searching for a platform provider, manufacturers should consider the following:

- ✦ Select a platform provider with at least 100,000+ users.
- ✦ Confirm that the platform provider offers all three delivery formats: online, webinar, and FTF services.
- ✦ Verify that the platform provider can integrate video, audio, and animation into your presentations. Avoid PDF presentations.
- ✦ Ask the platform provider for references from current clients about their course participation statistics.
- ✦ Review how the platform provider advertises their online courses and webinars. How do they build traffic and participation?
- ✦ Double-check that the platform provider has architects, specification experts, LEED consultants, and other design professionals on staff to develop your course.

THE SPEC SHAMAN

How to Get Specified On LEED v4 Projects

Building product manufacturers have several opportunities to get specified on LEED v4 projects. The LEED v4 rating system was launched in 2013. As of 2017, there are more than 90,500 commercial projects that are LEED certified with more than 5.8 billion certified commercial square feet. LEED is not going away, and any manufacturer who thinks LEED is a fad is misinformed. How can building product manufacturers leverage LEED v4 to get specified?

There have been significant changes made to the LEED rating system compared to previous versions, including a major overhaul of how building materials can contribute. Selecting "preferable" building materials – those with desirable human health and environmental attributes that deliver improved function, durability, and maintainability – has always been a significant component of LEED. Until recently, the focus within the LEED rating system was on single attributes, such as recycled content, locally sourced materials, and VOC content. Ratings covered a limited part of the materials' life cycle.

Understanding the health and environmental impacts of materials, as well as provide better access to tools and data, has allowed LEED to pursue an alternative approach. This is reflected in LEED v4 by delivering new materials and resources, credits that emphasize information disclosure, and materials optimization. The new LEED credits enable project teams to choose preferable products based on more robust, multifaceted information, including ingredient lists, human health hazards, and environmental impacts across the life cycle of materials. In addition, they provide incentives for manufacturers to improve their products. Examples of material transparency documents include Health Product Declarations (HPDs), Environmental Product Declarations (EPDs), Declare Labels, Cradle to Cradle certification, and several other USGBC-approved programs.

In 2016, the American Institute of Architects released a study entitled *Materials Transparency & Risk for Architects*. The study identified several crucial factors that architects should know about materials transparency. They include:

- **Transparency is the new normal.** There is a growing expectation that everyone involved in a building project – from initial design to occupancy – should have access to information on the potential health and environmental impacts relating to those products.

- **Materials transparency represents opportunities for architects.** These opportunities include competitive advantage, thought leadership, design innovation, and environmental and human health leadership.

- **New practices and procedures inherently present potential risks.** We accept that there is some risk in advocating for materials transparency and sharing composition information with our clients. With the passage of time, we will understand more about the risks. Nevertheless, best practices related to obtaining, using, storing, and transferring the information will help us manage them.

In addition, the AIA states, "The initiative to seek disclosure is driven primarily by a belief in the power of transparency to expose and thereby reduce unnecessarily harmful or risky choices. Architects can be in a strong position to encourage and incentivize disclosure, even if they lack the scientific expertise to interpret the data when it is disclosed. Whether or not it is used by architects, having the disclosed information gives building owners the option to engage independently qualified professionals to assess it and makes it possible for third parties to use it to provide better-informed guidance."

LEED Myths and Misinformation

There are multiple opportunities for manufacturers to get specified in LEED v4 and maximize their ROI. Unfortunately, there are several myths and misinformation in the marketplace about LEED v4. This misinformation can frustrate manufacturers and make participating in a LEED project seem impossible. Let's clear up several myths about LEED v4. One of the biggest myths that has circulated for years is that a building product can be certified by LEED or the USGBC. LEED does not certify products. If a manufacturer claims that they have a LEED-certified product, then they are lying. The USGBC does not certify or endorse products. There is no such thing as a USGBC-certified product. Another myth is that certain products are not allowed on LEED projects. LEED does not prohibit any product or technology. LEED does not ban products. LEED may set optional performance/environmental-based requirements that need to be met to earn points (such as for FSC lumber), however, LEED does not ban products like PVC.

Low-hanging Fruit in LEED v4

Although a super green building product might contribute to multiple LEED credits, we will examine the low-hanging fruit in LEED v4. Most manufacturers can contribute to several LEED credits in the Materials and Resources (MR) category and Indoor Environmental Quality (IEQ) category for New Construction BD+C projects. Manufacturers wanting to leverage their budget dollars to maximize ROI should review these strategies first.

Health Product Declarations (HPDs)

Top AEC firms in the U.S. are requesting Health Product Declarations (HPDs) from Manufacturers. Firms such as Perkins+Will Global, SmithGroupJJR, HKS Architects, and ZGF Architects are all encouraging Building product manufacturers to provide HPDs to be considered for product specification. Manufacturers who provide HPDs will be given preference over manufacturers that don't comply with these requests. HPDs are one of the easiest and most cost-effective ways to participate in LEED v4, the Living Building Challenge, WELL Building projects, Google Portico, and the mindful MATERIALS database. Any product manufacturer on the planet can contribute one point to LEED v4 projects with a LEED-compliant HPD. It's a foolproof way for product manufacturers to be part a of LEED v4.

The HPD is a document that lists the various chemicals and substances in a product and identifies the known health and environmental hazards associated with each chemical or substance. While this may seem like a relatively simple approach, developing a LEED-compliant HPD can be a frustrating process for manufacturers due to the complexity of supply chains and because suppliers oftentimes have concerns about disclosing trade secret information. The HPD is designed to overcome these barriers to product ingredient disclosure in a way that respects intellectual property concerns and includes offering tools to help work with upstream suppliers to collect the required information. Luckily, there are third-party consultants like Elixir Environmental who can help manufacturers develop LEED-compliant HPDs.

Product manufacturers with a LEED-compliant HPD can contribute points under the credit LEEDv4 BD+C *Building Product Disclosure and Optimization – Material Ingredients*. The credit is divided into three parts. HPDs can be used to fulfill the requirements for Option 1 and Option 2. Option 1 is for material ingredient reporting and Option 2 is for material ingredient optimization. Regarding LEED myths, many manufacturers are under the false impression that they cannot develop a LEED-complaint HPD because their product contains potential hazards, toxins, cancer causing chemicals, etc. This is simply false. All LEED-compliant HPDs can fulfill the requirements for Option 1 of this credit since it is simply a disclosure tool.

For an HPD to meet the requirements for this LEED credit, the threshold level for product ingredients must be at least 1,000 parts per million for Option 1 and 100 ppm for Option 2. In addition, all chemicals must be "characterized" – or must provide the percent by weight, and the role or function that chemical or substance fulfills in the product. Finally, chemicals or substances above the declared inventory threshold must be "screened" – or must be reviewed for hazards based on the HPD Priority Hazard Lists with the results disclosed.

AEC firms that are designing LEED v4 projects will typically have a Director of Sustainability, a Transparency Champion, or point of contact who will be engaged in receiving, reviewing, and helping select LEED-compliant HPDs. Most large AEC firms using HPDs for product selection will review the disclosures in detail to ensure that they meet the LEED v4 requirements. In the Division 01 section of their product specifications that discusses substitutions, firms might state that if an HPD is required for a specific project, a substitution will be rejected if it does not have an HPD that meets the quality requirements. Project teams will usually insert appropriate language in the Division 01 of their product specifications, documenting the fact that they are pursuing the LEED v4 Material Ingredients credit. They will include a very brief explanation of the credit and its requirements, including the link to credit requirements on the HPDC website.

Some manufacturers can provide full disclosure, while other manufacturers are concerned with intellectual property concerns, technical capacity, and supply chain communication gaps, which make full disclosure challenging for companies. Luckily, there are several resources available to manufacturers. Product manufacturers are highly encouraged to become members of the Health Product Declaration Collaborative (HPDC). The HPDC has several tools and education programs to assist manufacturers. Finally, third-party consultants such as Elixir Environmental offer services to help building product manufacturers develop LEED-compliant HPDs.

Sourcing of Raw Materials

LEED v4 is drastically different from LEED v3. Previously, product manufacturers liked to toot their own horn about their product's recycled content, that their cabinets were made from FSC-certified wood, and that their windows were made within 500 miles of a building project. Times have changed. Multiple LEED v3 credits have been combined into the LEED v4 BD+C credit *Building Product Disclosure and Optimization – Sourcing of Raw Materials*. There are two options for this credit, with a maximum of two points. For Option 1, product manufacturers can contribute to the credit if they publish a third-party-verified corporate sustainability report (CSR) and disclose several elements of their supply-chain practices, including extraction locations for raw materials. Acceptable CSRs include: Global Reporting Initiative (GRI) Sustainability Report, OECD Guidelines for Multinational Enterprises, and several other USGBC-approved programs. Option 2 of the credit is based on products meeting one or more responsible extraction criteria that include:

- ✦ Extended producer responsibility
- ✦ Bio-based materials
- ✦ Wood products
- ✦ Materials reuse
- ✦ Recycled content
- ✦ USGBC-approved program

LEED project teams pursuing Option 2 will review preliminary design concepts and identify opportunities to use and procure bio-based, qualified wood as well as salvaged and recycled-content materials and products covered by extended producer responsibility, especially for applications that use either significant quantities of materials or small amounts of high-cost materials. Wood products must be certified by the Forest Stewardship Council (FSC) unless they are considered reused, salvaged, or recycled. Project teams will track substitutions and change orders to ensure that replacement products meet the LEED credit requirements. Any product substitutions will be carefully reviewed by the team and contractor for compliance.

For credit achievement calculation, products sourced (extracted, manufactured, purchased) within 100 miles of the project site are valued at 200 percent of their base contributing cost. For credit achievement calculation, the base contributing cost of individual products compliant with multiple responsible extraction criteria is not permitted to exceed 100 percent of its total actual cost. Structure and enclosure materials may not constitute more than 30 percent of the value of compliant building products. There are multiple opportunities for manufacturers to achieve compliance with this credit. Please refer to the LEED v4 BD+C Reference Guide for more details.

Low-Emitting Materials

Another LEED credit that many product manufacturers may contribute to is the Low-Emitting Materials credit. The intent of the credit is "to reduce concentrations of chemical contaminants that can damage air quality, human health, productivity, and the environment." Many types of chemicals, both engineered and naturally occurring, are present everywhere. Volatile Organic Compounds (VOCs) are chemicals that are released into the air from numerous materials – some of them natural, human-made, plant-based, and from animals, including people. Prolonged exposure to high concentrations of some VOCs has been linked to a wide range of chronic health problems such as asthma, chronic obstructive pulmonary disease, and cancer.

The Low-Emitting Materials credit includes requirements for product manufacturers as well as project teams. It covers VOC emissions into indoor air and the VOC content of materials, as well as the testing methods by which indoor VOC emissions are determined. Different materials must meet different requirements to be considered compliant for this credit. The building's interior and exterior are organized in seven product categories, each with different thresholds of compliance. This is a detailed credit, so we will review the primary ways a manufacturer might contribute to the credit.

This credit uses the California Department of Public Health (CDPH) Standard Method for the Testing and Evaluation of Volatile Organic Chemical Emissions from Indoor Sources Using Environmental Chambers, v.1.1-2010 for the emissions testing and requirements of all products and materials except furniture. The method, widely recognized as a leadership standard for its stringent scientific criteria and detailed specificity, was developed through an open, consensus process. It uses the chronic reference exposure levels established by the California Office of Environmental Health Hazard Assessment, which include some of the most stringent criteria in use. For manufacturers who are new to product emissions testing, the first step is often the CDPH Standard Method.

To demonstrate compliance, a building product or layer must meet all of the following requirements, as applicable:

> **Inherently non-emitting sources.** Products that are inherently non-emitting sources of VOCs (stone, ceramic, powder-coated metals, plated or anodized metal, glass, concrete, clay brick, and unfinished or untreated solid wood flooring) are considered fully compliant without any VOC emissions testing if they do not include integral organic-based surface coatings, binders, or sealants.
>
> **General emissions evaluation.** Building products must be tested and determined compliant in accordance with CDPH Standard Method v1.1-2010, using the applicable exposure scenario. The

default scenario is the private office scenario. The manufacturer's or third-party certification must state the exposure scenario used to determine compliance. Claims of compliance for wet-applied products must state the amount applied in mass per surface area.

Manufacturers' claims of compliance with the above requirements must also state the range of total VOCs after 14 days (336 hours), measured as specified in the CDPH Standard Method v1.1:

- 0.5 mg/m3 or less;
- between 0.5 and 5.0 mg/m3; or
- 5.0 mg/m3 or more.

The General emissions evaluation applies to most products, even those where additional VOC content requirements also apply. All paints and coatings wet-applied on site must meet the applicable VOC limits of the California Air Resources Board (CARB) 2007, Suggested Control Measure (SCM) for Architectural Coatings, or the South Coast Air Quality Management District (SCAQMD) Rule 1113, effective June 3, 2011. There are several opportunities for manufacturers to achieve compliance with this LEED credit. Please refer to the LEED v4 BD+C Reference Guide for more details.

Environmental Product Declarations (EPDs)

We've reviewed several LEED credits that are considered low-hanging fruit for product manufacturers. Now we'll review a LEED credit that is applicable for manufacturers with larger budgets and resources. Building product manufacturers can contribute points in LEED v4 by developing an Environmental Product Declarations. If developing an HPD is taking baby steps, then developing an EPD might seem like running a back-breaking marathon. EPDs are created according to internationally harmonized standards and are third-party verified. This ensures that the results for your product are valid, ideally allowing direct comparisons to be made between your product and others in the marketplace. An EPD is like a nutrition label for foods, serving to effectively communicate the environmental performance of your product to your customers. Since the launch of LEED v4 in 2013, the state of EPDs in North America has been confusing, frustrating, and reminiscent of the Wild West for many product manufacturers.

For decades, several European countries mandated EPDs for projects. This gave large multinational companies a head start when the LEED v4 requirements were issued. In addition, EPDs can be very cost-prohibitive to develop for small- to medium-size manufacturers. In some cases, EPDs can cost tens of thousands of dollars to develop, as well as take several years. The amount of time, money, and other precious resources dedicated to EPD development has prevented them from becoming widely adopted like HPDs. However, advances in the industry will hopefully reduce their development costs and complexity for manufacturers in the future.

Manufacturers with compliant EPDs can contribute as many as two points for the LEED v4 BD+C credit *Building Product Disclosure and Optimization – Environmental Product Declarations*. Disclosures can contribute points based on whether they are a publicly available, critically reviewed LCA conforming to ISO 14044 (1/4 point). This is an industry-wide, generic EPD with third-party Type III certification in which the manufacturer is explicitly recognized as a participant by the program operator (1/2 point), or a product-specific Type III EPD (1 point). Manufacturers can contribute an additional point if their EPD demonstrates impact reduction for categories such as global warming potential, acidification of land and water sources, depletion of nonrenewable energy resources, and many other impacts.

In conclusion, EPDs are for companies dedicated to sustainable practices who want to analyze and reduce the environmental impacts of their products. EPDs are cost prohibitive for many manufacturers to develop, therefore HPDs have become a more accessible and affordable disclosure tool. A product manufacturer's road to sustainability is a work in progress and hopefully, one day, every manufacturer can publish an EPD.

LEED Product Documentation

Manufacturers need to have documentation that conveys how their product contributes to LEED. LEED product documentation ensures that you have the tools to get specified on LEED projects. The documentation is crucial to help specifiers with product selection. LEED product documentation should achieve several goals:

- ✦ Provide language to articulate the LEED v4 impacts associated with your product.
- ✦ List point-by-point primary and secondary associations of the product for all LEED credits.
- ✦ LEED product documentation should be distributed with as few obstacles to access as possible via the company website, brochures, and education courses.

Additional Specification Opportunities

LEED v4 is the most popular, successful, and widely used green-building rating system in the world. However, there are other green-building rating systems that may provide additional specification opportunities for product manufacturers. The Living Building Challenge and the WELL Building Standard are both becoming popular alternatives or additions to LEED v4.

The Living Building Challenge

The Living Building Challenge (LBC) is considered by many as the most stringent green building certification program in the world. LBC is a sustainable design framework that visualizes the ideal for the built environment. It uses the metaphor of a flower because the ideal built environment should function as cleanly and efficiently as a flower. The LBC is organized into seven performance areas called Petals. The Petals are very similar to LEED credit categories and include:

- ◆ Place
- ◆ Water
- ◆ Energy
- ◆ Health + Happiness
- ◆ Materials
- ◆ Equity
- ◆ Beauty

The standard set for LBC buildings is a high one: net-zero water consumption, net-zero energy consumption, and reduced construction materials, impact on people and the environment. As of 2017, only 15 projects in the world have achieved Living Certification. Yes, you read that correctly. Only 15 projects on the planet have received full LBC certification. The rest of the projects have received partial or no certification. The LBC is an inspirational program but too complex and cost prohibitive for most product manufacturers and design teams to work on. However, there might be specification opportunities for the brave soul who wants to collaborate on a LBC project.

To meet the criteria for the LBC, building products must not contain chemicals found on the Red List Building Materials. The Red List contains the worst-in-class materials prevalent in the building industry. The Red List contains the usual suspects, such as asbestos, bisphenol A, added formaldehyde, halogenated flame retardants, mercury, phthalates, and dozens of others. A building project may not contain any of the Red List chemicals or chemical groups. Although there is an exception for small components in complex products.

Declare Label

To assist designers specifying building products, the International Living Future Institute developed the Declare Label. A Declare Label answers three questions:

- Where does a product come from?
- What is it made of?
- Where does it go at the end of its life?

What's included on a Declare Label? The product and company name, end-of-life options, such as take-back programs, whether the product will end up in the landfill, is the product recyclable, etc. Next is the ingredients list reported by component. Finally, at the bottom of the label is the Declare Label identifier for the company, VOC information, and verification that the product complies with the Living Building Challenge Red List.

The Declare Label has been approved as a compliance pathway for the LEEDv4 BD+C *Building Product Disclosure and Optimization – Material Ingredient, Option 1*. The LEED v4 credit calls for the chemical inventory of a product to at least 1,000 ppm. Declare Labels that achieve a declaration status of "Red List Free" or "Declared" fulfill the credit disclosure requirements. The Declare Label is an excellent product disclosure tool. However, HPDs have been more widely adopted by design professionals. As of September 2017, there were 450 published Declare Labels and nearly 3,000 HPDs.

The Declare Label has more stringent standards than the HPD, is more expensive to develop and maintain, and has a limited niche in the construction industry outside of one LEED v4 credit. Product manufacturers receiving requests for Declare Labels should first consult with the interested AEC firm to determine if an HPD will suffice for their project. The limited number of LBC projects and stiff fees may impede many manufacturers from developing Declare Labels.

WELL Building Standard

The last green-building rating system we will explore is also the newest in the industry. Launched in October 2014, after six years of research and development, the WELL Building Standard is a program for buildings, interior spaces, and communities seeking to implement, validate, and measure features that support and advance human health and wellness.

WELL was developed by integrating cutting-edge scientific and medical research and literature on environmental health, behavioral factors, health outcomes, and demographic risk factors that affect health, with leading practices in building design and management. WELL also references existing standards and best practice guidelines set by governmental and professional organizations.

WELL consists of features across seven concepts that comprehensively address not only the design and operations of buildings, but also how they impact and influence human behaviors related to health and well being. Concepts in WELL are similar to LEED credit categories. The seven concepts include:

- Air
- Water
- Nourishment
- Light
- Fitness
- Comfort
- Mind

There are several opportunities for product manufacturers to contribute to a WELL project. We will examine one strategy based on the topics we have discussed thus far, specifically the development of HPDs. Project teams are rewarded for specifying products with HPDs under the Mind category and within the Material Transparency Feature. The Mind Feature aims to optimize cognitive and emotional health through design, technology, and treatment strategies. According to the International WELL Building Institute, just as consumers have a right to know the contents of the food they consume (whether to avoid allergic reactions or to make healthier nutrition choices), they should also have a right to know what is in the products and materials that make up the buildings they occupy. Demand for material ingredient disclosure at the consumer level pushes supply chain transparency and – even more importantly – supports innovation and green chemistry. Here is a breakdown of the Material Transparency Feature:

Part 1: Material Information

At least 50 percent (as measured by cost) of interior finishes and finish materials, furnishings (including workstations), and built-in furniture have some combination of the following material descriptions. (In order to contribute, the product must indicate that all ingredients have been evaluated and disclosed down to 1,000 ppm.):

a. Declare Label

b. Health Product Declaration

c. Any method accepted in USGBC's LEED v4 MR credit: *Building Product Disclosure and Optimization – Material Ingredients, Option 1*: material ingredient reporting

Part 2: Accessible Information

The following condition is met:

a. All declaration information is compiled and made readily available to occupants either digitally or as part of a printed manual.

In addition to the Material Transparency Feature, there are many opportunities for product manufacturers to contribute to WELL projects. Please consult the WELL website for additional information (www.wellcertified.com).

Material Health Disclosure Databases

So where do architects, designers, spec writers, interior designers, and other industry professionals find important disclosures like HPDs, EPDs, and Declare Labels? In the old days, project teams had to scour outdated product binders to locate critical information. Nearly everything is on the web today, making product specification much easier. We'll examine a few product databases that can benefit manufacturers.

HPD Public Repository

The HPD Public Repository is the authoritative source for published HPDs. When a manufacturer publishes an HPD using the HPD Builder, it is automatically uploaded to the Repository as a PDF file. HPDs that have been created by means other than the HPD Builder can also be uploaded to the Repository by the manufacturer. Once uploaded, an HPD is considered to be a "Public HPD." Uploaded PDFs are then searchable and available to be downloaded by users – architects, designers, project teams, property owners or any interested party. A simple search capability is available to aid in finding HPDs by manufacturer, product name, CSI classification or HPD version. This platform is free for designers to use and the definitive database for HPDs. Product manufacturers are highly encouraged to develop and publish their HPDs to increase product specifications.

mindful MATERIALS

HKS, an international architecture firm with 1,200 employees in more than 20 offices, saw a growing need to provide chemical content and environmental-impact information to project teams in a simple way. To answer this need, at the end of 2014, HKS developed mindful MATERIALS, an initiative that makes transparency and optimization information in product binders easily accessible to designers as they select products. The simplicity of the labeling system generated interest in the larger design community and HKS made the mindful MATERIALS resources publicly available to other design professionals and manufacturers.

mindful MATERIALS is a design-industry initiative that provides a common platform for manufacturers to clearly communicate transparency and optimization information for their building products. The challenge: How do manufacturers share product content information in a standard format, effectively and efficiently across the building industry? The solution: Through mindful MATERIALS, manufacturers enter product information directly into an online database, indicating which disclosure documents and certifications apply to each product. This database gives designers a single place to search for product information. The database further serves to inform a labeling system for products physically represented in resource libraries, placing this material attribute information at designers' fingertips. This platform is not only free for designers to find products, but also is free for product manufacturers to upload their product data.

Google Portico

Tech giant Google builds, leases, or renovates more than 100,000 square feet of property every Monday morning somewhere on the planet. Google evaluates all building products and materials through a rigorous screening process and uses benchmarks based on established industry standards that value product transparency and material health. Products that meet these strict criteria are available to be specified for Google design and construction projects around the world.

Google uses three screening methods to select building products – the Health Product Declaration (HPD), GreenScreen, and Cradle 2 Cradle Certification. Google's standards are closely aligned with the LEED v4 rating system. Product scores are indexed according to transparency and material health – higher levels of transparency and material health result in higher product scores. Google's global design and construction teams use the product's score to guide their material selection process. Here is their scoring system under the Healthy Materials Program:

Below Criteria: 1-3 points

Meets Criteria: 4-10 points

Exceeds Criteria: 11-16 points

Building products that meet or exceed the scoring system will be specified for Google projects. Most manufacturers find the easiest and most effective way to be considered for specification is by developing a

LEED v4-compliant HPD. Portico connects manufacturers and their supply chain to design professionals, providing a direct communications channel to request and provide detailed information about building products, streamlining the communications process, and saving time and money in the process. Manufacturers are highly encouraged to list their products on Google Portico.

Educating Your Team About LEED v4

As important as it is to educate architects about your products, it is crucial that your sales and marketing team understand the LEED certification process. How does your building product contribute to LEED v4? Manufacturers can lose out on jobs when they don't understand how the LEED certification process works. Building product reps should be well versed in what potential LEED credits apply to their building product. If your product reps don't know the difference between an EPD and an HPD, then how the heck will they get your products specified for a LEED project?

LEED certification training is beneficial for building product manufacturers by providing the necessary foundation for employees to understand the big picture. Not every employee has to be a LEED AP or LEED Green Associate; they only need to have a basic understanding of LEED v4 and how it applies to their products. Untrained staff can deplete your resources and distract your best people from urgent and important tasks. Luckily, there are free resources for building product manufacturers to train their employees about LEED certification. A high-quality, no-cost LEED v4 exam prep course is available to train your entire company about LEED at www.greence.com.

Conclusion

Invest your budget dollars in programs that generate a good return. Invest your time in people who are winners. How much money should you allocate to green-building opportunities, and how can you spend it wisely? Metrics, new customers, achieved goals, sales opportunities, and increased revenue can all be used to evaluate programs. Building product manufacturers don't have unlimited budgets. They need to justify their budgeting decisions based on ROI.

Manufacturers can gain market share, increase specification opportunities, and beat their competitors if they have the right resources. Developing an HPD should be the first step for any manufacturer who wants to contribute to LEED v4 projects. Picking the "low-hanging fruit" or easy LEED v4 credits is another strategy to implement. Producing LEED product documentation is a must for companies wanting to be involved in green-building projects. Listing your products in no-cost, green-building databases such as mindful MATERIALS and Google Portico is crucial for specification. Moreover, educating your employees about LEED v4 should be a no-brainer.

LEED can be complex, but it is surmountable. The competitive edge goes to manufacturers who lead. We can radically transform our economy by incorporating sustainable practices into our everyday lives and business. The LEED rating system has helped the design and construction industry accelerate the necessary transition to a sustainable built environment. The only way to ensure that we continue this transition is to implement the major strategies that we have discussed in this chapter. The time to act is now.

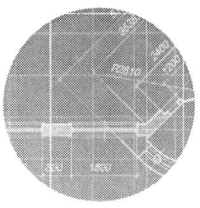

About the Authors

Ron Blank founded Ron Blank & Associates, Inc. (RBA) in 1985, providing a national architectural specification program to building product manufacturers. This program educates architects and other design professionals about building product technology in face-to-face meetings with specifiers, bridging the gap between design professionals and product manufacturers. His previous roles as a top sales and merger manager of an international construction product marketing company gave Ron the experience to develop training, territory management, professional-selling presentation skills, and insight into the importance of having products specified in an architect's master specification. RBA develops and manages hundreds of continuing education courses for product manufacturers, providing free continuing education credits through organizations like the U.S. Green Building Council (USGBC), Registered Continuing Education Program for Engineers (RCEP), and the Interior Design Continuing Education Council (IDCEC). Blank founded the CE Academy, allowing design professionals to receive 8 hours of credit in an all-day event. His webinar platform helps product manufacturers reach hundreds of architects at a time with their American Institute of Architects (AIA)-registered CE programs. Blank's passion is traveling the world, hunting, fishing, and loving his family and grandchildren.

Craig Haney founded IntroSpec LLC in 1988, which specializes in construction technology and specifications. Haney has more than 40 years of experience in the architecture and construction fields, 35 years of which have been dedicated to specifications and construction technology. He has consulted on projects covering a wide range of the built environment, both domestic and international. Craig has worked extensively with building product manufacturers, assisting them with understanding what design professionals need and getting their products specified. In 2010, Haney founded SpexPlus, Inc. to provide no-cost master specifications to design professionals, with system costs paid by construction product manufacturers. Haney is a Fellow of the Construction Specifications Institute and a CSI Certified Construction Specifier.

Brad Blank is an award-winning film producer who has lived with Indian tribes in the jungles of Panama, rafted the mighty Futaleufú River in Patagonia, and trekked the Southern Alps in New Zealand. He is the founder of GreenCE, the leading provider of free online AIA courses, GBCI courses, and free LEED-specific hour courses. GreenCE offers free LEED exam prep and LEED certification courses and collaborates with building product manufacturers to get building products specified by architects. He's produced building product videos – from the mountains of Montana to the deserts of Arizona. His education videos have been praised by the AIA, USGBC, and IDCEC. Brad obtained his MFA from the University of Miami graduate film program. He lives in the Pacific Northwest and enjoys walks on the beach, sunsets, and napalm.

To order additional copies of *The Spec Shaman*,

please visit us at

www.RonBlank.com

or contact us at 800.248.6364